WHAT OTHERS ARE SAYING

Marty White, Retired Audit Principal, a regional CPA firm

I've witnessed Tim Bishop's expertise and professionalism for years. As the partner in charge of auditing the company where he ran a mission-critical hedge program, I know he has the knowledge and skill to explain a complex topic like hedging in an understandable way. I read this book and it does just that.

Bob Moore, Chairman and CEO, Dead River Company

We had the benefit of Tim's unique skills, perspective and financial advice for many years. In a phrase, "Tim has been there, done that." This is a comprehensive and useful book, one which will truly assist specialized financial managers as well as operators who face commodity price and supply risks.

Heather Bergeron, Managing Director, Dixie Asset Management

I read Hedging Demystified and I thought it was great—so user friendly. It answers so many questions that a new face to hedging may not think to ask until it's too late.

Joe Smith, VP, an energy marketing and distribution company

Tim Bishop capitalizes on his expertise to provide an overview of hedging of commodity price risk in a straightforward manner that doesn't require prior knowledge or a strong financial background. This book will be beneficial to both newcomers to the subject area as well as those wanting to broaden their understanding.

Jordan Ness, Fuels Trader, Chemoil, a division of Glencore

The texts are laid out in a way that makes the relevant issues easy to understand and separate from one another in spite of dealing with an already complex topic. …I particularly enjoyed the chapter on basis, I thought the layout was excellent.

Charlie Hahn, CFO, Dead River Company

Tim Bishop has managed to take a very difficult topic and make it understandable for all. I particularly like the numerous illustrations and the ability to "toggle" from chapter to chapter as key topics are revisited. I will be using this book as a key reference tool.

HEDGING
DEMYSTIFIED

*How to Balance Risk
and Protect Profit*

TIM BISHOP

OPEN
ROAD
PRESS

Publisher's Note

This publication is designed to provide helpful information about the subject matter covered. It is sold with the understanding that the publisher is not engaged in rendering professional hedging services. If expert assistance is required, the service of an appropriate professional should be sought.

This print edition, published in 2019 as a service to readers, contains the content that was published in e-book form in 2014 as *Hedging Commodity Price Risk: A Small Business Perspective*. The only changes to that content were made to convert the e-book with hyperlinks to a print format, upgrade the cover, and change the title.

Most references herein to commodity futures exchanges pertain to the CMEGroup. Other exchanges may differ. Exchange rules are always changing, so check the rules of your exchange for current information.

Published in Thompson's Station, TN, USA by Open Road Press.
http://hedging.openroadpress.com
First Edition

Library of Congress Control Number: 2019900604
Print edition ISBN: 978-0-9856248-7-3
E-book edition ISBN: 978-0-9856248-0-4

Professionally edited by Sandra J. Judd
Cover design: tatlin.net

CONTENTS

Section IV: Hedging Risks

Section V: Hedging Wrap-up

ILLUSTRATIONS

FOREWORD

As someone who has worked in the energy industry in a variety of roles for over 34 years, I have frequently been involved in activities associated with the hedging of commodity price risk. This exposure has covered a variety of job roles and applications, including over ten years as a consultant providing assistance to a range of small to large domestic and international organizations. During that time, I often observed quizzical looks and blank faces when the topic of commodity hedging was explored at more than a cursory level. Confusion was particularly evident when hedging results were explained (i.e., what happened and why?).

Tim Bishop's book *Hedging Demystified: How to Balance Risk and Protect Profit* is an excellent tool for those who want or need to explore this topic in more detail, in particular, for those who have limited to moderate experience in this subject area. It's always important to keep in mind that not hedging for whatever reason (even due to lack of knowledge or understanding) fundamentally represents a choice. The impact of a hedging program for these types of companies can be crucial to their long-term health.

The underlying rationale for hedging commodity price risk is generally well understood, essentially representing a type of insurance aimed at preventing, or at least limiting, the potential for large unexpected losses due to commodity price exposure. Although this high-level understanding is widespread, the phrase "the devil is in the details" certainly applies. Taking the necessary steps to implement an appropriate and effective hedging strategy consistent with the risk profile of a company and its stakeholders can be challenging. Since exposure to commodity price risk is widespread across a range of industries and geographies, the potential application of hedging is extensive.

Not surprisingly, the understanding of hedging is generally strong for practitioners, though these same people can be challenged or perhaps disinterested in communicating their understanding to others. When hedging results are worse than expected (or better than expected, though the questions are typically fewer in this scenario), the hedger's explanation can be spiced with technical jargon, leading to more confusion than clarity. In smaller organizations, this understanding is typically concentrated in a few people. If an interested party doesn't understand the general principles and underlying rationale and activities associated with hedging, comprehending hedging strategy and results will be much more challenging.

This is where Tim Bishop's book fits in nicely, as it provides a broad spectrum of potential readers a strong foundation to better understand this vital topic. Although there are a plethora of books that deal with hedging, this book does an excellent job of explaining the fundamentals in a simple, conversational style that doesn't require prior knowledge or a strong mathematical or financial background. The author provides simple and clear quantitative examples covering various commodities. These examples help enhance one's understanding of hedging strategies and their potential implications. Lastly, his small-company experience leads to a unique focus that recognizes that the responsibilities are often shouldered by a select few individuals in a smaller company.

Although Bishop's book can be readily understood without prior experience with hedging, there is still a substantial amount of pertinent information for readers who already have a solid understanding of the topic. He covers some of the more important and relevant facets of hedging. For example, included is a good discussion of "basis risk," which can often be a major component of the underlying risk that needs to be hedged. Hedging of basis risk can pose more of a challenge than hedging the underlying commodity price risk itself. If the impact of basis risk is ignored, the hedging results can be much different than expected. This section will better equip the reader to address this issue if it is pertinent. Even if the reader is already familiar with basis risk, this section will provide a good refresher to this important subject.

Bishop also wades into the arcane world of accounting for hedges, which can often lead to the reported results differing substantially from the basic underlying operating performance of the company. (Note this assertion comes from a non-accountant!) Although the detailed accounting for hedging and derivatives is a complex topic and a thorough discussion is well beyond the scope of his book, the author uses his hedging experience and strong accounting background to introduce some important concepts that can help readers understand what circumstances could lead to unexpected financial results. Knowing how these types of anomalies arise can help ensure that reported financial results do not overshadow the fundamental performance of the company.

In summary, Bishop has written an excellent introductory book on the hedging of commodity price risk, which can offer benefits to a wide range of readers, from those with little to no experience in hedging to those with more familiarity with the topic.

Joe Smith
Vice President
An energy marketing and distribution company

PREFACE

Commodity price risk. The term sure sounds academic. However, if you're trying to run a business and you're facing this risk, it can turn what looks like a good year into a not-so-good year, or a great year into a disaster. Hedging that risk well will stabilize your business and help you sleep better at night. With the proper understanding, effectively managing commodity price risk is well within your reach.

Changing commodity prices can bankrupt businesses tied to those commodities. Depending upon the size of the business, thousands of dollars can evaporate in mere seconds due to events unrelated to the business and out of its control. I've seen it happen. Perhaps you have, too. A weather event, a political event, or a who-knows-what event changed the value of a commodity used in your business—to your detriment. Suddenly, your business's value declined. And it had nothing to do with running the daily operation.

Textbooks often have difficulty teaching the practical application of an abstract topic like hedging. It's time someone took the mystery out of it. That's where *Hedging Demystified: How To Balance Risk and Protect Profit* comes in. This is not an academic book by either definition of the word "academic." You won't become buried in minutia. You won't find words like "alpha," "beta," "delta," "straddle," "spread," or "naked call option." What you will find is what you need to know. This book was written by a businessperson for a businessperson.

If you're out there rolling the dice, hoping that changes in commodity prices, interest rates, foreign currency exchange rates, or weather won't sting you again this year, your anxiety is justified. Yet there's no reason to wait for the ax to fall. This book explains the basics of hedging in easy-to-understand language. It demonstrates how the tools and the markets can work to reduce risk.

Whether you've already dabbled with a hedge program or you're looking at the possibility for the first time, in this book you'll learn the pitfalls and opportunities of hedging, so you'll know what to expect once you're in the game to stay. *Hedging Demystified* is chock full of information and ideas sure to stimulate improvements in how you manage price risk. It's helpful for anyone who wants to better understand hedging.

Small businesses are not immune from the carnage that fluctuations in commodity prices can bring. They may also lack the capital to absorb wild price swings. Their margin for error is slim, yet their size may present unique challenges to hedging the risk. While large, multinational corporations can hire staff specifically to hedge risk with financial derivatives, smaller businesses often must look within to find a person with the right aptitude and temperament to manage their risk. This book will accelerate the learning process.

In over fourteen years of hedging price risk, I've found that many people connected to the business with "a need to know" struggle to understand hedging concepts, mechanics, and risks— regardless of their position in or around the organization. Yet, until now, they couldn't simply go online to pick up a book on hedging they would readily understand and then read up on it. Well, now they can!

Professionally edited, *Hedging Demystified* had some serious tire-kickers perusing its pages before it went to press. I sought advice from experts in their field—seasoned hedgers, commodity brokers, suppliers, bankers, marketers, accountants, finance gurus, tax specialists, generalists, lay people, and small businesspeople alike. The feedback was clear: risk is on everyone's radar. Managing it can be challenging, but it must be done and it must be done well.

Since you cannot engage in a discussion about hedging without understanding some measure of theory, I will introduce the concepts through conversational language and practical examples. The examples demonstrate time-tested techniques, regardless of the commodity. I have defined each of the more challenging terms in a glossary in the back. There's also an index, so you can navigate to the text topically. Finally, the list of website addresses acts as a gateway to additional content to enhance your learning.

So, let's sit down for coffee. I may write on the napkin a few times to illustrate some of the more complicated pieces, but beyond that, let's enjoy a practical discussion that will open your eyes to some new possibilities on how to protect your business's value from commodity price risk.

SECTION I

Hedging Basics

Until you know your risks, you won't be able to hedge them properly.

CHAPTER 1

The Markets

Welcome to the virtual market, where you can trade all
sorts of commodities without any of them changing hands!

Before we dive right into hedging, let me introduce you to a new marketplace. You'll learn much about it in the pages ahead, but it is important to establish up front that hedging will require you to think about more than just the traditional marketplace you've been accustomed to for years.

We'll call the traditional market the physical market. It's where tangible goods move about—in exchange for cash, of course. It's how most people think about business transactions. You want something I sell? Give me some money and I will give it to you. That's the traditional market at its core.

The new marketplace is a bit different. It anticipates prices in the future and it operates with its own set of rules. Yet it is connected to the traditional market, in that it trades the same commodities. We'll refer to this market as the futures market.

"Commodities?" you ask. Yes, you know them: corn, soybeans, wheat, cattle, electricity, natural gas, crude oil, gasoline, milk, sugar, coffee, gold, silver, copper, and platinum, among others—the basic building blocks of an economy. Even debt, currency, and weather act as commodities in some businesses. Many companies use commodities, and their prices tend to oscillate based on the laws of supply and demand. Supply and demand are tied to any number of unpredictable factors, either real or anticipated, that can tip the balance. When this happens, price, the great equalizer, moves to reestablish equilibrium.

You will encounter discussions in this book about both the physical market and the futures market for the same commodity. Each market has its own set of prices and its own pool of buyers and sellers. Yet, **when these two markets come together, they give birth to hedging.** The effective hedger establishes positions of opposing risk in each market. When combined, the risks associated with the positions in the two markets essentially cancel each other out.

A physical market is a collection of buyers and sellers who transact with the express purpose of exchanging a commodity. In a futures market, by contrast, the exchange of a commodity can be a rare occasion. We'll define a futures market as an aggregation of traders who are willing to commit to delivering, or taking delivery of, a specific commodity at some point in the future for a certain price. The futures market will allow them to back away from those delivery commitments before they arrive. Most traders need this flexibility or they won't participate.

The purpose of the futures market is more about establishing future prices than it is about arranging future deliveries. Establishing future prices helps businesses plan, manage risk, and actually transact orders before delivering the products they sell. **When a business strategically unites the physical and futures markets as choreographed dance partners, risk has been escorted to the door and invited to spoil someone else's party, if not their bottom line.**

Some buyers and sellers of a commodity will participate in both the physical market and the futures market. The futures market, however, will have a much larger pool of buyers and sellers than the physical market, some of whom are not really in a business related to the commodity they are trading. They are trading futures because they think they can make money, whether or not they have an offsetting risk in their portfolio. Yet it matters not. They help others in that market who have a direct business interest in the commodity at hand by providing additional trading partners for them. When there are more traders in a given market, pricing is typically more transparent and more equitable because bidding is more active and more competitive.

The commodity itself may be the only connection between the physical and futures markets that trade it. Yet, sometimes, those markets are tied together in business deals. For example, you may contract with a vendor to purchase a commodity based upon its futures price. When you transact that purchase, you are still trading in the physical market even though your price is predicated on other people's trades in the futures market.

These two markets can also be linked together when a futures contract expires. In order to honor the commitment to deliver under the futures contract, an exchange of the commodity for cash will occur. But, again, this transaction occurs in the physical market, with the futures market merely determining the commodity price.

Although the term "futures market" implies singularity, in reality the market is complex and fragmented. For our purposes, we might rather think of the futures market as a collection of alternatives for trading commodities for future delivery. You'll discover a variety of these hedging tools as you dig deeper into this book.

Now that you've been introduced to the futures market, I'd like you to consider some of the reasons for hedging, and what hedging really is. Then we'll delve into how the futures market works to establish an effective hedge on commodity price risk.

CHAPTER 2

Why Hedge?

Doing nothing is a decision—sometimes a regrettable one.

What is the purpose of hedging? Why trade in the commodity futures market? Doesn't this activity come with its own set of risks?

The benefit of trading in this market, for those who understand it and use it wisely, is that trading can reduce the overall risk of doing nothing. Effective hedging ultimately protects a business's asset value and net worth. It stabilizes the earnings stream, bringing predictability out of the unpredictable. It can help you stay in business for the long term.

Price Risk Scenarios

Consider the following:

1. A wholesaler purchases a large quantity of gasoline at a fixed price. The market price could decline before he liquidates his inventory. What can he do to protect the value of his inventory, and therefore the value of his business?

2. A heating oil distributor contracts with his customers in June for delivery of heating oil the following winter at either a fixed price or a price not to exceed a certain level. The price of oil may go up, but the distributor's selling price for these gallons cannot, since he has already committed to a fixed price or a capped price with his customers. How does the distributor protect his profit margin on the sales of these fixed-price and capped-price gallons?

3. It is early in the growing season. A wheat farmer who has planted fifty thousand acres is concerned that there may be a glut of wheat on the market at harvest. She sees that she can lock in a fair price now, four months before harvest. This will at least help her cover some of her costs and ensure she can pay the mortgage. If she waits, maybe she'll get a better price, especially if the United States brokers that deal they've been working on with Russia. However, if that falls through, surely the price will decline. How does the farmer secure the profit margin on some of her wheat in order to pay the bills?

4. A real estate investor purchased a large office building six months ago. He financed the purchase at a variable interest rate. Most of the building is now leased over a reasonably long term. If interest rates go up substantially, the rent will not cover the increased debt payments. He'd like to convert the financing to a fixed rate, even though he'll pay a higher rate, because the rent is sufficient to cover the payments at the higher fixed interest rate. He can then be assured of a steadier stream of cash with a higher likelihood of meeting his financial obligations. How does the investor fix his interest rate?

5. A manufacturer uses large amounts of copper in its process. The business has just secured a large contract for one of its premier products. If copper prices increase beyond a certain threshold, the business will lose money on this contract. How does the manufacturer prevent a loss of money on this contract due to potential increases in the price of copper?

6. A US farming operation has just signed a contract to sell some of next summer's harvest in Europe. It will collect its sales proceeds in Euros, and its contract has fixed the price. If the value of the Euro weakens against the US dollar, the farming operation will receive less compensation when it converts the sales proceeds into its own currency. How can the operation protect itself from losing money due to a weakening Euro?

7. A regional airline has just instituted a price change to cover recent increases in jet fuel costs. It doesn't want to increase rates again in the near term, yet management is concerned about the possibility of additional price spikes for jet fuel in the coming months. What steps can the airline take to

ensure that a further rise in the cost of fuel doesn't necessitate another fare hike?

8. A Midwestern farmer has a pending deal to acquire more acreage and growing capacity from an estate. He would like to commit this acreage to corn next year, and the futures prices suggest more than a handsome return on this investment, thanks to a deal the US government has just negotiated with China. However, what if another development between now and then causes the price of corn to decline? How can he lock in that price today before committing time and money to expanding his corn crop?

9. It's summer, and there's a glut of heating oil on the market. Meanwhile, long-term weather forecasts are suggesting a very cold winter, causing prices for wintertime heating oil to trade nearly 30 cents per gallon higher than the current market price. An oil supplier has substantial unused storage capacity, and he can borrow money now at very low cost. If he could lock in the high selling price for delivery sometime next winter, he'd be willing to buy some oil now because he knows he can make a lot of money on the deal. In fact, he is estimating a 35 percent annualized return on the capital he would invest. He knows he can sell the product to some distributors at favorable prices when cold weather arrives. How can he confidently proceed with the purchase now while capitalizing on the high selling price for winter oil?

In each of the above cases, the businessperson is concerned about an adverse change in the price of a commodity that will cause him or her to lose money. Each has a commodity price risk. **A business has a commodity price risk if either an increase or a decrease in the price of a commodity will reduce the business's overall value.** When a material risk exists, other financial obligations will often demand that a business find an effective risk management solution. The futures market, or some other hedging mechanism, can help contain the risk.

Grappling with Risk

Have you ever heard the old axiom "you don't get something for nothing?" Well, it's true—never more so than with managing commodity price risk. There's a cost to hedging that risk, including the cost of managing and executing an effective program. Hedging cost also includes a forgone benefit (i.e., an opportunity cost), which is usually more material than the costs of administering the hedge.

The opportunity cost presents an interesting dilemma. With changing commodity prices, if you don't get a bad result, you're usually left with a pleasant surprise. And the stakes can be very high. If you don't mind risk and you don't mind jeopardizing the value of your business, then you might rather save the opportunity cost and go it alone—and stop reading any further about this hedging nonsense.

However, if you're like most businesspeople, you'll want to make sure you live to fight another day. You've made a long-term investment in your business, and you anticipate the payday down the road when you exit the business—or pass it on to your heirs. You may conclude, as most do, that the opportunity cost is an investment in your long-term livelihood.

Risk and reward are indeed lifelong partners. You can't have one without the other. When you ask one of them to leave you alone, its companion waltzes right out the door with it. Yet that's okay, because you're in business for the long haul. When you hedge your commodity price risk, you still bear enough business risk to earn a handsome reward, but you eliminate the nasty commodity price risk you could do without.

Sometimes, risk may be right under your nose without you knowing it. It may sneak in undetected until telltale signs surface. It may expose itself unashamedly, stealing away a large percentage of annual earnings that you just can't miss. Or, it may hibernate. You may discover it when something good happens. The change in the price of a commodity may actually increase your business's value. Take note, however: behind unexpected gains, an unmanaged price risk may be lurking. What may benefit your business today could come back to bite it in the future. Good news sometimes portends catastrophe.

One way or the other, risk must be unmasked. If you don't know and understand your price risks, you'll never be able to hedge them. **This is the single most important rule of hedging: know your risk!**

Once you understand your risks and resolve to manage them, your hedging costs will invariably be less than the cost of doing nothing when the price of a commodity tied to your business changes in a dramatic and adverse way. Although the cost of eliminating all risk is to exit the business and forgo its financial rewards, most prudent businesspeople will make a reasonable assessment of risk and then decide how to best mitigate that risk.

What's your business risk? Do price swings in certain commodities threaten your bottom line? If you take steps now to assess your risks, you'll be in a better position to manage them. Don't wait until it's too late! Your payday may never come if you don't manage risk well.

CHAPTER 3

What Is Hedging?

Hedging is simple. Its details, however, will confound you.

Hedging has been around for many years. I know that because my mother supported traders of Aroostook County potatoes in the 1960s from a potato house in Houlton, Maine. You may have heard the term tossed about in the business news, perhaps tied to the word "fund" and to a scandal, with a visual of a white-collar criminal escorted from a courtroom in handcuffs, headed to a more modest dwelling than the one he was accustomed to. Hedging can mean different things to different people. Many skeptics may equate it with gambling or greed. Yet, for those with otherwise unmanageable risk, it's the white knight who saves the damsel in distress.

In the context of commodity price risk, **we'll define hedging as any technique used to transfer or mitigate the risk through a specific course of action.** Usually, a business does this by entering into a transaction that offsets the risk associated with another transaction.

Consider the following. If a company purchases oil at a fixed price without any firm sales commitments, and the market price of oil falls before it can liquidate the inventory, it will lose money. As the price of oil drops, so too will the value of the business's inventory. Commodity price risk is looming.

The business can hedge this risk by finding another party who will agree to fix a selling price for the oil. By its very nature, the futures market offers willing and ready buyers to would-be hedgers. "Selling" the oil on the futures market will establish that fixed selling price. It will create a position in the futures, or "paper," market that opposes the business's position in the physical market. I will explain this in more detail later in this chapter.

Often, hedging involves giving up an opportunity—as well as its associated risk. If the company in the prior example chose not to sell futures contracts in the futures market, it could make a lot of money, were the price of oil to go up. The value of its inventory would then increase. This forgone benefit is the opportunity cost.

Nevertheless, when a company chooses to hedge a commodity price risk, a third party steps in to absorb the risk. Whatever the third party's circumstances may be (and these circumstances are irrelevant to the hedger), the third party judges itself to be in a position to take on the associated risk, or to offset it with an opposing risk it may already own.

When a business enters into a hedging transaction, it is trying to secure a profit or to limit a loss. It is attempting to reduce uncertainty in its financial performance. Stakeholders, such as bankers and investors, want predictable earnings. Hedging may entail forgoing additional gains in order to secure a lesser benefit. Regardless, it is ultimately designed to reduce risk. **Because of the perception of forgone profits, hedging may come with some internal angst. And since greed often wages war against the need to hedge, a disciplined approach becomes the hallmark of an effective program.**

Another way to describe hedging is to consider what it is not. Hedging is not speculation. Speculation is trading in the markets without having a risk to offset. You may have industry knowledge that leads to insights and hunches about price direction, but unless you have a risk to transfer, any trading on that knowledge is mere speculation that the price will move in your favor. This type of trading is more akin to "playing the markets." Although a lot of money can be made, much can be lost as well. Hedging and speculation are sisters with opposite personalities.

Hedging Marketplaces

Commodity futures exchanges exist to provide an efficient and ready market for hedgers. Since the government regulates them, traders gain some level of comfort that the markets operate fairly and with appropriate structure. Commodity futures contracts are standardized so that market participants understand what they are trading. Contract specifications address product type, quantity, grade, and delivery location. They also specify month of delivery (e.g., March 2014 delivery of 5,000 bushels of Chicago #2 soft red winter wheat . . . for more details, see http://www.cmegroup.com/trading/agricultural/grain-and-oilseed/wheat_contract_specifications.html). Market participants are prescreened in order to qualify for trading, and this includes a full financial review for assessing creditworthiness. When prices change on open futures contracts, the exchange governs the flow of funds between traders.

Other trading opportunities exist with so-called over-the-counter trading partners. Over-the-counter markets may allow you to customize the specifications, although standard over-the-counter instruments have become commonplace. Without the governance of a regulated exchange, however, knowledge of the trading partner's creditworthiness and ability to perform are significant considerations. (For more on these counterparty risks, see Chapter 16.) Some businesses may be able to transfer commodity price risk to their customer base, or to another business partner, like a financial institution, a vendor, or an insurance company.

I'll explain the markets in more depth in Section II.

What Does It Mean to Sell a Commodity Forward?

When I first began to learn about futures contracts, I struggled with the concept of selling something I didn't first buy. How can you sell what you don't own?

However, **the word "sell" in this context is a misnomer. When you "sell" a futures contract, you are really making a commitment.** You are committing to deliver a certain quantity of a certain commodity at a certain price to a certain location at a certain future time. (This commentary pertains to traditional futures contracts that are premised on the delivery commitment. You may find some futures contracts that do not have a delivery requirement and are settled financially.) Even the commodity contract itself has certain specifications as to quality. This commitment, however, is conditional, and most people who trade in the futures market make conditional promises. The only component of the commitment that isn't conditional is the price. Until the contract expires, you have the ability to back out of the delivery commitment by purchasing another contract just like it. For instance, if you sold one wheat contract, you can cancel the commitment to deliver under that contract by simply purchasing one identical wheat contract.

The term "purchasing" is also a misnomer because when you "buy" a futures contract, you are committing to take delivery of a certain quantity of a certain commodity at a certain price at a certain location at a certain future time. Yet no goods have changed hands.

These commitments are made irrespective of whether the person making them has the ability to deliver on them. They are simply financial transactions that most often occur apart from any delivery of a physical commodity. And, after you've backed out of your commitments, you're left with the only binding piece—the price, which will result in you either collecting from the market or paying into it, depending upon whether or not your selling price exceeded your purchase price.

The price of the futures contract is determined by an open marketplace of unconstrained buyers and sellers. The price is theoretically the price at which a willing buyer and a willing seller would transact based upon a delivery at a predetermined future time and location. It is the market's perception of the fair value of a commodity at some point in the future.

Selling a commodity forward may sound good in theory, but in practice, there are other complexities. As discussed, the delivery of the commodity usually never happens—at least not in the futures marketplace. **Optimally, from a hedging standpoint, the commitment to deliver under the futures contract will be canceled when the physical commodity that was hedged is priced and delivered.** Comparing the purchase and sale prices of the offsetting futures contracts will render a futures gain or loss. Adding this hedging result to the gain or loss incurred on the physical commodity that was hedged should approximate a result that was anticipated when entering into the hedge.

How Does Hedging with Futures Work?

When a company "sells" a commodity in the futures market, it is entering into a financial obligation. In effect, it is executing a contract, referred to as "paper" (though no paper exists, since no one is signing a physical document). With this contract, the hedger is agreeing to a fixed price and a fixed quantity. He is establishing a position. Someone else in the futures market has taken the other side of his position, and it really matters not who it is, because the futures exchange handles the flow of funds and the offset of all positions. For a further explanation of how to offset futures contracts, see Chapter 4.

The position that a hedger establishes is usually in reverse of the physical commodity that he is hedging, in order to nullify its price movement. For example, a crude oil refiner who has bought oil, or a farmer who has grown corn, will sell a futures contract for the same commodity, likely in the approximate month each will deliver the physical product to its customers. A trading company that has sold, or otherwise committed a fixed price to a third party for, a product that the trading company does not yet own, such as coal or gold, will purchase a futures contract.

After each futures position is established, prices will continue to fluctuate until the futures contract expires. The hedger will want to close the position when he delivers his physical product so he isn't subjected to the price fluctuation thereafter. Otherwise, he'll incur additional gain or loss on the futures contract, which will no longer be matched to a physical position. If this happens, once again he'll have a price risk. However, this time, it will pertain to the futures contract, not the physical commodity.

Ideally, the change in the futures price will mirror the price change of the physical commodity that the hedger is hedging, thus eliminating any gain or loss that occurs

while holding the combined physical and futures positions.
When he sells his product, he should earn the profit margin
anticipated when he entered into the hedge. The hedger locked
in both the cost and the selling price when he simultaneously
executed the original deal and opened the futures position.
When ownership of the hedged item passes to the buyer, he will
again simultaneously exit the futures position.

Steering Profits

If a rancher owns one hundred head of cattle, but they're not yet
ready for prime time, he may want to hedge all of that price risk
by selling one hundred head of cattle in the futures market. After
all, their selling price will fluctuate until he finds a buyer and
agrees to a price. In the meantime, the futures market provides a
mechanism to lock, or fix, the selling price.

The rancher, turned hedger, may already be able to estimate
the actual cost associated with his one hundred head of cattle.
Since the cost is already fixed, fixing the selling price will also fix
the profit margin. All that needs to occur for the hedger to earn
that margin is that he needs to locate some buyers, deliver the
cattle at market prices, and collect the cash.

Typically, a sale to an unrelated buyer in the physical market
will occur at the prevailing market price. That price will usually
approximate the price of the near-term futures contract. The
rancher's cattle may be purchased by one buyer in one
transaction or by many buyers across many transactions. He will
want to begin reducing the size of his futures position as he
begins to receive commitments from buyers at established prices
in the physical marketplace. When all of the cattle the rancher
has hedged have been committed at fixed prices to physical
buyers, the rancher should reduce his hedge position to zero.

The selling price in the physical market will vary from the
selling price locked in earlier on the futures market. The
difference in those selling prices will be substantially offset by a
gain or loss in the futures market. That same gain or loss added
to the profit margin earned on the physical sale should
approximate the originally expected margin. And when the
selling price for the physical cattle is adjusted by the gain or
loss on the futures contracts, the post-hedge, all-in selling price

Illustration 3.1

Hedging Margin

	Physical Market	Futures Market	Combined
Assumptions:			
Live heads of cattle	100		
Expected cost of feed, labor, delivery, etc.	$57,000		
Expected cost per head	$570		
Futures price per head		$975	
Potential margin per head	$405		
Step #1: Sell into futures market			
Selling price		$975	
Step #2: Sale of physical (months later)			
Sell price of physical	$915		
Futures price on sale date		$915	
Margin without hedge	$345		$345
Gain on futures		$60	$60
Margin with hedge			$405
Recap (per head):			
Intended margin			$405
Margin without hedge			$345
Margin with hedge			$405

should approximate the price at which the rancher originally sold the futures contracts (plus or minus any basis differences, as explained in Chapter 13).

What happens if the price of cattle plummets before delivery? A $60 decline per head could have cost the rancher $6,000 ($60 x 100 heads). However, since he locked in his selling price in the futures market, he'll collect the difference there and restore his margin to the anticipated amount. If, on the flipside, the price skyrockets, the rancher will still make the same margin. When he locked in his selling price, he also locked in his margin.

While it is true that by hedging he gave up the potential to make more money, he knew the price could just as likely have declined. He didn't have the financial wherewithal—or the stomach—to absorb a substantial price decline. So, he is satisfied with a fair return and a good night's sleep.

In practice, cattle futures are sold by weight, subject to grade qualifications, and in contract lot sizes. We'll ignore those complications in this example, as shown in Illustration 3.1.

A hedger who "sells" a physical commodity into the futures market receives "paper" that will represent a negative quantity. In the above example, the rancher holds a futures position of negative one hundred cattle (in actuality, he holds a futures position equal to the number of pounds his cattle weigh, rounded to the closest multiple of whole contracts based on the standard contract size). If one is 100 percent hedged, the quantity of the physical product added to the quantity on paper equals zero. From a financial perspective rather than a legal one, the hedger owns no head of cattle. He has substantially eliminated his price risk.

Price Correlation

Did you notice I inserted the word "substantially" in the prior sentence? If the change in the price of the futures does not correlate with the change in the price of the physical cattle, there will still be price risk. And the futures market and the physical market are different. They each have their own unique prices and price changes.

If the selling price of a physical commodity is based on the futures index, or if actual delivery occurs under a futures contract (if the contract for the commodity in question allows for it), price risk is not a concern, provided the hedge is timely. However, if the physical selling price is determined by any other means, the correlation in price changes between the futures market and the physical market will be a factor.

Based on historical trends, there is usually close correlation in price change between the physical markets for a commodity and its futures markets. Otherwise, hedging with futures contracts would have limited benefit because those contracts would not adequately curtail the price risk. Because price correlation is often a consideration in a hedge program, let's consider it further.

Correlation is an observable characteristic when comparing two distinct price indices. Price indices may change similarly, or they may not. One may go up $2, while the other goes down $1. Or, one may go up $1.11, while the other goes up $1.12. The degree to which the changes vary, or are similar, is called correlation. The latter example has a better degree of price correlation than the former.

Here's an analogy that demonstrates the principle of price correlation:

The crowd has gathered around two identical shimmy poles, with two contenders ready to scale to the top. Once the gun sounds, they dash to the poles and begin their ascent. One of them, however, is heavier than the other and immediately lags behind. Quickly, as the crowd roars its approval, the smaller contender snatches the banana atop the pole, a prize for his swift climb. Eventually, contender number two also makes it to the top.

The next round pits the winner with a contender much more equally matched to his size and speed. The two scale their poles virtually in unison. When they reach the top, the replay official needs to go behind the curtain to determine who grabbed the banana first!

When you're hedging commodities, you'll want a hedging instrument whose price moves in tandem with the price of the commodity you are hedging. The pace of the second set of contenders correlated much better than the first. If they were price indices, they'd make better hedging partners.

In addition to describing the relationship between two price indices, correlation is also an actual measurement. One can quantify correlation over time. A correlation factor of one (1.0) means the two indices change in lockstep with one another. The closer a correlation factor is to one, the better chance the hedger will achieve the result he expects and wants. If the price of the product a person is hedging and the price of the instrument he is using to protect its value do not correlate well, the hedge results will be less reliable and less predictable.

In general, aligning product specifications in a futures contract more closely with those of the product at risk helps achieve better price correlation and a more effective hedge. For example, hedging the value of Australian sheep with Midwestern cattle futures would be inadvisable. Those products have no reliable price correlation. Neither do diesel fuel and gasoline, even though they are siblings born from the same barrel of crude oil.

There may be location differences between physical products and hedge instruments. Those differences can create significant correlation issues. See the further discussion about basis in Chapter 13.

While a hedger's goal is to reduce overall financial risk, poor price correlation of a hedge instrument can actually increase risk. Choose your hedging tools wisely! We'll now look more closely at these tools.

SECTION II

Hedging Tools

You can't cut a board with a hammer. Nor can you pound nails with a hacksaw.

CHAPTER 4

Futures

Although the future never arrives, you can still plan for it.

The most common tool for hedging risk is a futures contract. We touched on futures earlier. In this chapter, I'll describe the regulated futures marketplace where futures contracts are traded and then better define the attributes and characteristics of a regulated futures contract.

What Is a Commodity Futures Market?

A commodity futures market is an aggregation of buyers and sellers of the same commodity for delivery in future months. It exists to provide liquidity to its participants, allowing them to trade at will at a price determined by the market itself. The market is liquid because it has enough participants willing to take the other side of any trade at any time. If a wheat farmer wants to sell some of his product in advance of the harvest because the future price would lock in an acceptable profit, he can do so because there will be a party in the futures market willing to buy wheat contracts.

Some participate in the futures market to reduce their financial risk by transferring it to another party. Those participants are hedgers. Other participants speculate on the price direction of particular commodities by taking positions that they believe will make money. They do not have an identifiable financial risk that they are trying to offset. Although some traders believe speculators unfairly manipulate commodity prices, in most cases they are helpful to a futures market because they enhance liquidity for hedgers.

Except during extremely unusual and infrequent market disruptions, a trade is always possible in a liquid futures market, but its price may not always be what one would expect or hope for. Rather, a commodity's price will reflect the collective opinion of the market. The traditional forces of supply and demand certainly influence price direction. Depending upon the commodity, political events and natural phenomena, such as military strikes, terrorist activities, drought, and hurricanes, can also have a significant bearing on price. However, actual trades in the market ultimately establish commodity prices. As an example, see the gasoline futures trades at http://www.cmegroup .com/trading/energy/refined-products/rbob-gasoline_quotes_ timeSales_globex_futures.html.

If the wheat farmer in our prior example chooses to wait for a higher price, it may never come—even after he harvests his crop. He cannot hold the wheat indefinitely, until the market offers a higher price, because his crop has a limited life. Agricultural businesses have a high degree of risk due to factors such as weather, which can make them rich or bankrupt them. Hedging a portion of each year's crop can help cover some operating costs, should the unthinkable—or the unimaginable—occur.

In reality, the farmer does not sell his wheat crop to the party on the other side of the trade in the futures market. In fact, he never knows the identity of the party who purchases the contract. Rather, the farmer is agreeing to deliver the contract quantity of wheat at the expiration date of the futures contract at a place specified in the contract. Upon delivery, he will collect cash based on the price at which he sold the futures contract. The buyer is making a similar promise, except he will be taking delivery.

Actual delivery, however, may not (and most often does not) occur. Instead, contract holders will close their futures positions before the futures contracts expire, recording a gain or loss on the futures trade. Simultaneously, they will typically deliver their physical product at the prevailing market price, or at a predetermined committed price.

What Is a Futures Exchange?

A futures exchange is the structure of a futures market. It is an organization comprised of qualified clearing member firms. It exists to regulate the market, to facilitate efficient trading, to manage the exchange of funds between market participants as prices fluctuate, to manage the settlement of contracts, and to provide a knowledge base of pertinent information for its members and other interested parties.

A properly regulated exchange effectively eliminates traders' concerns that they may not be paid for gains. It accomplishes this by pooling and managing the credit risk of all clearing member firms, and by requiring immediate cash exchanges on adverse changes in the value of futures positions. One position holder's loss is another position holder's gain.

A clearing member firm is one of the select financial institutions that has sufficient financial strength, controls, and structure to qualify with the exchange. The following webpage shows the current clearing members of the CMEGroup, the behemoth of futures exchanges: http://www.cmegroup.com /tools-information/clearing-firms.html. The exchange has rules and procedures to ensure financial performance. It imposes capital investment requirements on each member commensurate to each member's risk. The exchange then monitors each member's financial strength and credit procedures going forward.

Anyone who trades on the exchange, whether to speculate or to hedge, must do so under the auspices of a broker and a clearing member firm. A broker is likely affiliated with a clearing member firm, if not the clearing member firm itself.

Clearing members will assess the creditworthiness of their clients using exchange criteria as well as their own guidelines. They will work with the exchange to manage the flow of funds to and from the entity that ultimately bears the gain or loss from the trades. That's you, if you trade in the market! They'll be careful to select their clients wisely because the clearing member firm is ultimately liable to the exchange for any funds owed by their own trading clients.

If a clearing member firm defaults on its cash obligations to the exchange, the exchange will absorb the default. In all likelihood, however, because of the oversight and significant capital requirements for its participants, the exchange will not experience a default by a clearing member. The exchange is funded by fees collected from its member firms.

What Are Futures Contracts?

Futures contracts are the primary trading instruments on a regulated exchange. I touched on them in the prior chapter. They are referred to as "paper." Yet, with an exchange-traded futures contract, no two parties sign a document laying out the terms of the contract to which they will be bound. Regardless, a legally binding contract does indeed exist until the contract is offset, as explained below.

A brokerage agreement provides the legal framework that binds position holders to their futures contracts. Most contracts are executed with a phone call to the broker or through online trading software, and the broker will confirm a client's trades and report the resulting contract holdings on daily statements thereafter.

Futures contracts are specific to product and delivery month, and although you'll never file one in your legal drawer, you can look up the contract specifications on the Internet, since the contracts are standardized. For example, here's the CMEGroup's contract specifications webpage for live cattle: http://www .cmegroup.com/trading/agricultural/livestock/live-cattle_contract _specifications.html.

Each contract trades with its own set of prices. Typically, an exchange will report the high, low, opening, and closing prices each day for each such contract. Check out https://www .cmegroup.com/trading/agricultural/livestock/live-cattle.html for live cattle trades.

In futures terminology, to buy a contract makes the purchaser "long" the contract. To sell a contract is to go "short." **A futures contract is closed, or offset, by trading an identical contract in the opposite direction of the initial trade.** To close a wheat contract that was first sold, the contract holder would buy another wheat contract (i.e., the same product specification, the same quantity, and the same month of delivery). To close a wheat contract that was initially bought, the contract holder would sell an identical wheat contract.

Futures contracts also have standard quantities. For example, one crude oil contract contains one thousand barrels. This facilitates efficient trading, but it may also slant the playing field in favor of larger firms with plenty of quantity to trade.

What if you need to hedge only 350 barrels of crude oil? You'll need to find another alternative to manage the risk effectively, and you'll likely find one with an over-the-counter trading partner. I'll describe that further in Chapter 6. Not all hedging challenges can be met on a regulated exchange. Yet there are more hedging tools than readily meet the eye. Anyone with a material price risk will do well to continue their quest for the tool best suited to their needs.

A futures contract will typically expire sometime before the last day of the contract month, depending upon the commodity. After all, it is a futures contract. Just as tomorrow never arrives, so too with a futures contract. Expiration could occur just prior to the contract month or somewhere in the middle of it, again, depending upon the commodity. For example, market partici-pants can trade a June contract for gasoline up until the last day of May. If you hold a position in the contract on the last day of May, and you do not execute a trade to offset the contract, you will need to make a provision to either deliver or accept delivery of the commodity specified by the contract, depending upon whether you are short or long the contract.

Delivering on a futures contract is such a rare and impractical occurrence that most traders will want to avoid it—and most brokers will work with you to prevent it. You must understand the ramifications, which might vary depending upon the commodity, before you find yourself stuck with a contract after expiration. If you are, consult with your broker and other industry players on how best to satisfy the delivery requirements.

At any time, a chain of monthly contracts for the same commodity will list on an exchange. The exchange determines the number of months to be listed for each commodity, and which calendar months will be listed.

How Do You "Pay for" Futures Contracts?

A position in a futures contract, in and of itself, costs nothing. If you exit the contract at the same price you acquired it, you have no gain or loss. Sure, you will incur a commission for your broker to execute the trade, track your activity, and advise you, but these fees are typically modest. However, when you take on a futures position, you are entertaining the potential for significant gain or loss on the contracts themselves. That gain or loss will occur as the futures price of the commodity changes.

From a cash flow standpoint, the exchange on which you traded the contract and the clearing member whom your broker is using to manage your trades are only really concerned about the losses you may incur, or more specifically, your ability to pay for those losses. That's why they check your credit thoroughly before accepting you as a client. That's also why you must post collateral for your every position. This collateral is referred to as margin.

When the price goes against you, you incur losses, and those losses are paid for by your margin account. When the balance in your margin account drops below a certain required threshold, you must replenish it. You will immediately receive a "margin call" from your broker.

Margin calls are mathematically computed based upon your current account balance, which reflects the gains and losses you have incurred, and the exposure of the open positions in your account as determined by exchange regulations and your clearing agent. As an example, margin requirements for gold are found here: http://www.cmegroup.com/trading/metals/precious/gold_performance_bonds.html.

Your clearing member firm's review of your credit will help determine your creditworthiness, and therefore how much cash collateral you will need to post when you enter into positions. Expect a periodic review of an audited set of financial statements and a request for some banking references. If you don't have good credit, you'll need to post more collateral in this "pay to play" arena.

Each day, your positions will be "marked to market," which means your futures portfolio will be repriced based upon the daily settlement prices of the futures positions you hold. The exchange establishes all settlement prices, which approximate market value at the close of the trading session. Any gains in your positions will increase the cash balance in your margin account; any losses will reduce it, and could lead to a margin call from your broker. In typical arrangements, margin cash can flow back to you if your positions have moved sufficiently in your favor. Your daily account statement from your broker should apprise you of any cash that is available to you at your request.

If you cannot afford to underwrite substantial losses before you deliver on and collect cash from your physical product commitments, you may not be in a position to hedge on a regulated exchange. You may need to ask a bank to step in for you. Or, you may need to rely upon your supplier. These third parties will likely command an additional cost for this service, as compared to dealing directly with the futures exchange.

Illustration 4.1

Gasoline Futures Curve

Per Gallon Price as of 12/26/13

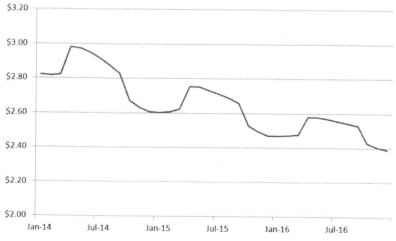

The Futures Curve

If you plotted the monthly prices for gasoline futures onto a graph, chronologically from left to right, and joined the plot points with a line, you would see that each price differs from the others. The line will ebb and flow into the shape of a curve, as shown in Illustration 4.1. A graph like this is known as a futures curve. Certain factors influence the formation of a futures curve. Some of those factors are common to all commodities; some are unique to each.

You may be dealing with a commodity with supply or demand affected by seasonal factors. For example, agricultural commodities have a growing season and a shelf life, both impacting supply. Cold weather and increased traffic in summer months both affect demand for a variety of energy products. Severe weather events can disrupt supply, perhaps even demand, for many commodities.

There may be other extenuating influences on a commodity's supply and demand. The futures curve for each commodity will reflect those factors. For example, the gasoline curve shown above reflects not only increased demand in summer months, but also the costlier summer grade of gasoline mandated by law. For a sample curve of another commodity, see the wheat curve in Chapter 9.

There's good reason to anticipate that the futures curve would increase over time, absent seasonal or other extenuating circumstances. After all, if we want to own a commodity in the future, we could buy it today and store it until we need it. Doing so would incur costs to carry the inventory, including capital costs (measured in the form of interest expense), logistical costs (to handle and relocate the commodity to its temporary storage site), storage costs (whether the inventory owner rents or owns the storage facility), and maybe even insurance costs to protect the inventory against risk of loss before liquidation. The future cost equivalent of today's purchase should include a premium to pay for these services, rendering a higher value for tomorrow's commodity.

In reality, however, the futures curve is determined by an open market of buyers and sellers. When you move from the classroom to the street, some economic theories will not translate as expected. Not all futures months are created equally. **The variability in monthly prices is an important dynamic for anyone who uses futures contracts to hedge**

risk. The easiest way to monitor the curve for your commodity is to review daily settlement prices on a screen like this CMEGroup webpage, which lists the daily settlement prices for gasoline: http://www.cmegroup.com/trading/energy/refined-products/rbob-gasoline_quotes_settlements_futures.html. If you attempt to visualize the curve based on real-time activity, you'll be misled, because contracts for some months trade less often than do others. Learning how to read your commodity's curve is a key facet to recognizing hedging opportunities as well as hedging challenges. We'll look into this further in Chapter 9.

Price Discovery

A futures exchange helps inform the marketplace of the value of any given commodity at any given time because it provides an active market, with trades at agreed-upon prices, and publicly discloses those prices. One need go no further than to view a CMEGroup webpage showing the pricing for various months of a commodity to assess its perceived value in the future. Knowing the value of one's commodity can then provide the basis for business decisions. For example, on December 26, 2013, the market price for January 2015 delivery of gasoline was $2.60, as shown in Illustration 4.1.

CHAPTER 5

Options

Need some price insurance? Shop the "options store,"
where anything can be assigned a value.

What Are Options?

An option is premised on another contract. And as you might imagine, it does present you with a choice! You can choose to either buy or not buy (or sell or not sell) the underlying contract. Whether you have an option to buy or to sell depends upon the type of option contract you hold.

Options exist for many forms of financial instruments. However, for purposes of our discussion, we will refer to options for commodity futures contracts. Most regulated exchanges that offer commodities futures contracts also offer options on those contracts. The options contracts on a regulated exchange are executed and documented much like the futures contracts are.

Why Options?

The risk profile of most business transactions works like a teeter-totter, with the two parties to the transaction on opposite ends. When the price moves in one direction, Party A benefits while Party B suffers. When the price moves in the opposite direction, the teeter-totter reverses. Party A is now losing ground while Party B is gaining ground. Party B now benefits at the expense of Party A.

Let's think of this type of risk profile as a bi-directional price risk. For every winner, there is a dollar-for-dollar loser. Based on the law of averages, anyone who plays on this teeter-totter will lose some benefit at least 50 percent of the time.

For example, if you've sold your winter wheat on a futures exchange at a fixed price and the price of wheat goes down, you've just received a benefit. Congratulations! You have a higher selling price than the market currently offers. For the trader who bought the wheat in anticipation of rising prices, the price decline is a setback because she could have purchased the wheat at a lower price had she waited. There's one winner and one loser (when considering only this transaction). Trading in futures is a zero-sum game. A futures contract, in and of itself, has a bi-directional price risk profile.

But what if there is a winner and a loser only when prices move in one direction? When the price moves in the opposite direction, neither party is at risk. We'll call this a one-directional price risk.

Such is the case with a capped price on a commodity like heating oil. When a customer participates in a capped-price program, he benefits because he can purchase his oil at the cap price when the market price is higher. Yet he pays the market price just like everyone else does when it is lower than the cap. While he may have spent some money for the cap-price privilege (after all, nothing is free), the cost of that protection is invariably less than if he'd committed to a fixed price and then the market crashed. The difference between the price when he entered the cap program and the price at delivery may be several times greater than the cost of his "insurance," or the premium he paid to participate in the program. He wins in both cases. He has protection against higher prices, and he can still purchase at lower prices, should the market price decline.

As a marketer, if you want to provide your customers with a "best of both worlds" scenario like this one, you need an option to secure the one-directional price risk. **An option will allow you to choose the optimal of two prices: the price embedded in the option or the current market price.** If, instead, you try to hedge a one-directional price risk with a futures contract, which is bi-directional, it will work only 50 percent of the time. If the price goes against you, and the value of the futures contract becomes negative, you'll have a potential catastrophe on your hands. You won't have an offsetting business benefit to absorb the futures loss. That's when an option should have been used. We'll look at examples of these scenarios in Chapter 7.

An option allows you to acquire a futures contract at favorable pricing, should you need it. The option itself will not subject you to a futures loss. In exchange, you'll pay anyone who will sell (i.e., write) you an option to assume that risk for you. **The premium you pay quantifies the value of the risk you are transferring. Unlike a futures contract, with its un-limited potential for loss, the loss potential for someone who buys an option is limited to its premium.**

Options ratchet up the level of complexity significantly, but they are important hedging tools because they address one-directional price risk.

How Do Options Work?

Options come in two basic types: an option to buy and an option to sell. An option to buy is a call option. An option to sell is a put option. Unlike trading a futures contract, where you simply commit to a fixed price at delivery and no cash changes hands at inception (with the exception of margin cash), when you trade an option, you pay (or collect) a premium, which is the marketplace's assessment of the value of the risk transfer when the option is traded.

An option's identifiers point to its underlying commodity contract. For example, if you wanted to secure the option to buy crude oil at a certain price, you might purchase a crude oil Dec 100 call option. Dec refers to December, the delivery month of the futures contract associated with this particular option. Because the December futures will expire near the end of November, this option will also expire before December. Options usually expire a few days before their underlying futures contracts expire to facilitate efficient expiration of the underlying contracts.

The number 100 in the above example is the option's strike price. When you exercise an option, you do so at its strike price.

Any exchange-traded commodity futures option must specify a product, a delivery month, a strike price, and a type (whether call or put).

The holder of an exchange-traded option can either trade it or exercise it. If the option is exercised, it is converted into the applicable futures position. Exercising a crude oil Dec 100 call option would result in the holder acquiring a long crude oil futures contract priced at $100.

An option is "in the money" if it has intrinsic value, which means that if the option were exercised, the resultant futures contract would immediately show a gain. In our example, if December crude is trading at $102, the call option has an intrinsic value of $2 per the unit of measure inherent in the contract. Since the crude oil contract is measured in barrels, the option has an intrinsic value of $2 per barrel.

If an option is traded rather than exercised or expiring worthless, it is typically valued at its intrinsic value plus an additional amount that represents the "time value" left in the option. This time value diminishes as the option approaches expiration.

Pricing Considerations

Option markets typically experience fewer trades than futures markets, so the premiums paid for options can be slanted in favor of the person who is writing (selling) the option. Mathematicians have developed formulas to compute option values for a variety of assets. In measuring the time value of an option, those formulas take into account interest cost and the inherent risk in the underlying asset, as indicated by the range of price movement in that asset (its volatility). An option's style (e.g., American, European, or Asian) will also influence its price. For further information on option styles, see this Wikipedia webpage: http://en.wikipedia.org/wiki/Option_style.

Although option-pricing models are beyond the scope of this book, here is a Wikipedia webpage for the formula to compute the value of an option on a futures contract, the so-called Black-76 model: http://en.wikipedia.org/wiki/Black_model. Since option quotes can be erratic due to the complexity of pricing models, the subjectivity of the assumptions that feed those models, and the seller's favored position in an illiquid market, this formula can be useful to test hedging scenarios and to assess the fair value of specific options before trading them.

Because option pricing is complex and other deals may be competing for a market maker's attention, it can sometimes be difficult to price and trade futures options favorably on a regulated exchange, especially in small quantities. Some over-the-counter market makers will write you options that look just like exchange-traded options, but at better value. If these options have identical specifications, you may be able to transfer them to your exchange, thereby consolidating the accounting, funds flow, and credit risk with your exchange-traded positions.

CHAPTER 6

OTC Instruments

*Don't try to force a square peg into a round hole. Instead,
go find a round peg.*

In the prior two chapters, I've described hedging tools that trade
on a regulated exchange. Sometimes, however, those tools may
not adequately address your hedging needs. It's then that you'll
want to look "over the counter." Over-the-counter (OTC)
instruments can accomplish hedging goals in a similar fashion to
exchange-traded instruments. Yet they exist in a different realm
with its own characteristics. Understanding how these markets
operate will help you determine how to approach them. Let's
look further.

What Are Over-the-Counter Markets?

Over-the-counter (OTC) markets refer to marketplaces that
provide hedging alternatives to regulated futures exchanges.
Banks, insurance companies, vendors, and other businesses
familiar with a particular commodity create these markets. Even
customers can be a source of hedging alter-natives. Essentially,
any entity that is interested in helping you manage price risk
(because it profits them) and is in a position to do so can be a
hedging partner.

Historically, OTC markets have had less structure than
regulated exchanges, although many of them utilize standard
contracts. Regulations imposed in the United States after a large
business failure and a bailout of a financial giant in 2008 have
imposed more structure to OTC markets there. **OTC markets**

are important, as they can accommodate hedging needs that regulated exchanges cannot.

Banks offer the advantage of already understanding your creditworthiness, and they typically come with deep pockets due to the regulations imposed on financial institutions. You already have a significant business relationship with your bank. In addition, you may already have established the necessary credit to allow them to underwrite your hedging program. In the US, banks are required to report hedging transactions to regulators, which may alleviate your reporting burden.

Insurance companies understand risk. This is how they have survived, if not prospered, over the years. They understand weather-related risk particularly well (clearly, weather can influence many commodity prices). Because of their actuarial expertise, an insurance company may be in a good position to assess your risk, assign a value to it, and offer you a hedging alternative.

Your vendors know your industry perhaps better than any prospective trading partner does. In addition, they already have a business relationship with you. If they sell the commodity you want to hedge, they may be able to help you achieve your hedging goals without the use of a separate hedging instrument. This could simplify hedge management and accounting for the results.

When considering the various OTC hedging alternatives, it may be difficult to know the real value of your risk and the payouts of different scenarios under each proposal. You should compare the alternatives to one another and to the cost of hedging more conventionally on an exchange, if that method exists. If a partner is going to assume your commodity price risk in addition to your credit risk, that partner will expect good compensation.

What Is a Swap?

Whereas a futures contract is the typical financial instrument traded on a regulated futures exchange, a swap is the instrument of choice in over-the-counter markets. **From a hedging standpoint, the effect of a swap is similar to that of a**

futures contract, but a swap is always settled financially. There is never delivery of an underlying commodity.

Unlike futures contracts, swaps usually are settled based upon an average of the daily settlement prices of a commodity during the period specified in the swap. The unit settlement value of the swap is calculated by comparing that average daily price to the "swap price" agreed to by the parties when they entered the transaction. The original swap agreement also stipulates who pays whom and what quantity applies to the unit settlement value to determine the total swap payout. As with futures contracts, one party's benefit is another party's cost. For further explanation of how swap payouts are calculated, see the example of the swap trade at the end of this chapter.

Because a swap settles ratably across the period of time it is hedging, it is typically self-managing. You don't need to buy or sell contracts on a daily basis to remove your hedge. The averaging aspect of how the swap settles provides an effective, straight-line hedge. That may be just what you need.

The relationship between over-the-counter parties is often governed by a standard document called the International Swaps and Derivatives Association, Inc. (ISDA) master agreement. This is a legal document executed by two parties to establish a trading relationship. It spells out the standard legal details of trading in over-the-counter financial derivatives. A separate executable document will spell out the specifics of each deal struck under the master agreement.

Most swaps are not altered, revoked, or settled early. They are held until they settle as originally specified. You can alter the effect of a swap by entering into another one or more swap agreements designed to achieve the desired result when taken together with the first swap. Adding the values of the multiple swaps should approximate the revised hedging strategy.

Any entity that can provide you a trading alternative in OTC markets is called a market maker. Creative market makers can tailor swaps to achieve about any result conceivable. There are even market makers who will write an option on a swap if you want one. Due to the complexities of swaps and their options, make sure you understand any deal before committing to it.

Customization of OTC Deals

With an OTC market, you are able to customize the hedging instrument, tailoring it to address the specific risk at hand. There are a number of reasons that this might be necessary.

Smaller companies may lack the critical mass to hedge on the scale required in larger markets. Sometimes the quantity of a standard futures contract may exceed a company's quantity at risk for any given month. Exchange-traded contracts can't be split into smaller increments, which can pose a problem with smaller risk pools. OTC markets won't leave smaller players out in the cold like regulated exchanges will.

You may want to customize a contract for product specification reasons rather than for quantity. Although standard specifications may approximate your product's specification, this still may not be close enough to prevent price correlation issues from arising. Finding a partner to write a contract to your product's specification removes that risk.

You may instead find a partner who will offer you a derivative based on the difference between an exchange-traded commodity and your product. In that event, you can utilize the benefits of the regulated exchange to manage the bulk of the risk with futures contracts and use swaps to hedge the correlation (basis) risk. See Chapter 13 for a further discussion of basis risk.

Sometimes hedging requirements are so specific that the only alternative is OTC. Hedging a weather-related risk to the weather readings of a small airport near your business is one example. An interest-rate swap for a loan is another.

Credit Considerations

Although recent US regulatory changes have created a class of credit management for certain OTC trades that looks more like that of regulated exchanges, credit is still a primary distinguishing characteristic of OTC markets. There remains an OTC trading classification where credit risk lies solely between trading partners. Since market makers may no longer have an exchange on which to pool your credit risk, and they may lack daily reimbursement of your loss positions, they'll really need to understand and be comfortable with your credit standing.

The same should apply in reverse when a market maker could owe you money. Hedging with an OTC partner may mean all your counterparty credit risk lies with one entity. Have you checked their balance sheet and read their financial statement footnotes? If that partner cannot make good on their financial obligations, a positive hedging gain at their expense will be of no value to you. You'll be left to absorb the entire loss associated with the commodity price risk you were hedging. **Make sure you perform some sort of credit check on your hedging partners.** It's as important for you as it is for them. High-profile credit defaults of the past attest to the potential severity of the risk.

We'll look at counterparty credit risk further in Chapter 16.

Pricing Considerations

Trading prices are a significant determinant of financial results. With an OTC market, you may be narrowing your possibilities for hedging your risk. **One consequence of a narrower market is less price competition.** Furthermore, in some cases, an OTC deal may be intertwined with other business aspects that make the pricing difficult to measure and compare to the alternatives.

It's common that a swap will be valued substantially lower than its trade price only days after trading it, with no perceptible change in the market. That's because the trading partner has embedded a profit in their price, a provision that rewards them for assuming your risk and accommodating your need to hedge. Just how much profit is reasonable is anyone's opinion, and yours will be much different from theirs! It's a rude awakening to realize that you might have been able to secure a better price elsewhere. **Examine your alternatives before you commit to a swap.**

Intangible factors other than price may be driving your choice of hedging partner. Those factors might include the business relationship, simplifying the management of the hedge, the need to pool quantities with other similarly sized businesses, limitations on cash flow, or simply understanding the economics. Although these may be valid reasons for trading with a familiar face, don't lose sight of how much the arrangement is really costing you.

An Example of an OTC Swap

To illustrate how swaps work, consider an example using propane as the commodity. A propane marketer may offer his customers a fixed-price contract annually. He will want to lock in an acceptable profit margin to prevent a loss should the price of propane rise. Propane trades so infrequently on a regulated exchange that most hedgers will need to find an OTC market maker to swap risk with them.

The propane marketer contacts a supplier, who is familiar with, and typically writes, propane swaps with its clientele. The supplier agrees to provide a fixed cost for propane by executing one or more swap agreements with the marketer. These agreements are merely financial instruments. Any arrangement whereby the marketer acquires the physical product to satisfy his fixed-price propane obligations with his customers is separate and distinct from the swap agreement. He may purchase the product from the supplier providing the swap, or he may purchase it elsewhere—it matters not.

In June, assume the marketer requests a price quote for twenty thousand gallons each in October, November, and April, and forty thousand gallons each in December, January, February, and March. Note that the exchange's standard contract size for propane is forty-two thousand gallons, but the marketer does not anticipate that much volume in any of the months. Since he is trading over the counter, his quantities can be any amount, assuming his trading counterparty will accommodate him. The contract they mutually execute will specify his unique quantities.

When the supplier looks at the marketer's requirements, he may quote an entire strip (e.g., one price and one contract for October through April), or he may quote each month in the strip separately and settle them monthly. For our example, he'll trade the entire strip at once, but each month will settle separately.

He offers a price of $1.00 per gallon, which the marketer accepts after comparing the supplier's offer to several others he has requested from other market makers (including a bank, another one of his suppliers, and a larger, unrelated company that deals with several energy products). He is satisfied that the $2.00 sell price he is offering his customers will cover the raw commodity cost plus the cost of landing the product in his customers' tanks and leave him with an acceptable profit margin to cover his overhead and contribute to his bottom line.

October rolls around. Propane supply has been tightening, and the cost of the commodity has risen substantially. The price index referenced in the swap agreement averages $1.45 when taking all of the business days for October into account. To settle the October portion of the swap agreement, the supplier will pay the marketer $9,000 (45 cents per gallon times 20,000 gallons). When the marketer purchased propane to deliver gallons to these fixed-price customers, he paid a comparable price for the raw commodity. Therefore, the proceeds from the settlement of the swap restore his margin to the originally anticipated amount.

The marketer receives comparable per-gallon payouts in the months that follow until February arrives. A particularly warm January and the impending end to cold weather has relaxed supply and lowered propane prices. Additional supply coming online from an unexpected source applies additional downside pressure on the commodity price.

When the February portion of the swap is settled, the average price across the month of February was only 90 cents per gallon. Because the average price for the month was lower than the swap price of $1.00, the marketer owes the supplier $4,000 (10 cents times 40,000 gallons for February). Yet the marketer's expanding margin on cost declines (since he's been buying the physical commodity at prevailing market prices) provides the necessary funds to pay the supplier what is due him under the swap agreement. Again, the swap payout adjusts the actual margin to arrive at a margin that approximates the originally intended amount.

****

We've now laid the groundwork to consider several practical examples of hedging. While by no means exhaustive, these examples should illustrate how the tools described in this section will help protect you from commodity price risk. They'll also strengthen your understanding of what we've already covered. Thereafter, we'll look at some other risks associated with hedging.

SECTION III

Hedging Applications

Even the right tools won't help if you don't know how to use them.

CHAPTER 7

Forward Sales

A deal is not a deal until you deliver on it.

For our purposes, forward sales are pre-delivery agreements that a vendor makes with its customers to provide some measure of price protection to them, usually at a fixed price or at a price not to exceed a certain amount (a capped price). Because the vendor is agreeing to limit the customer's exposure to price increases, it is assuming this price risk and should consider hedging it.

Fixed-Price Sales

Often, marketers will offer to sell their product well before delivery. Their selling price can be based on an index and float with the market until the order is filled, or their selling price can be fixed when the sales contract is executed. Sometimes cash will change hands before delivery, but not always. The transaction is completed when the product is delivered and the customer pays for it.

When a marketer extends a contract for future delivery at a price that is fixed when the contract is executed, he has assumed a price risk. The marketer anticipates earning a margin on this sale, but does not yet know what the cost will be. If he could establish this cost with certainty, he would essentially fix his profit margin. However, if he does not lock down the cost, it could either increase, thereby reducing the profit margin, or decrease, which would expand the margin.

Banks and other creditors want borrowers with predictable cash flow who can meet their debt obligations. Fixing the margin would stabilize this borrower's cash flow. It would also prevent a catastrophic loss should the commodity cost increase substantially.

How can a marketer fix the cost of a fixed-price sale? There are several ways.

First, he can contract with another company to supply, at a fixed cost, the product needed to fulfill the sales contract, an arrangement known as a fixed forward contract. Because there is a transfer of risk from the marketer to his supplier, the supplier will expect additional compensation. The premium he charges the marketer will reduce the marketer's profit margin. The marketer is also dependent upon the supplier for timely delivery to ensure fulfillment of the marketer's commitment to his customer.

Another technique to manage this price risk is to set aside physical product. This is not a very efficient method because it ties up capital dollars to carry the inventory. It may also introduce some record-keeping challenges. Furthermore, it may be difficult to set aside gallons earmarked for just one class of trade. Yet the market may allow enough profit margin to compensate the marketer for the cost of carrying the capital investment. When delivery occurs, the marketer will need to adjust the inventory earmarked for the fixed-price sale. If the record keeping is manageable, this technique is feasible.

A more common hedging technique for a fixed-price sale, however, is to buy futures when the customer and the marketer agree to a quantity and a selling price, and to sell (close, offset) the futures when the marketer's cost for the product that will satisfy the customer's commitments is established, which often occurs at delivery. The advantage of using futures contracts is that the marketer can readily liquidate them. He can trade them online immediately, or with a quick call to his broker. The futures market will also provide instant pricing information, and will drive the effect of price changes into his financial statements. That may provide more transparency in financial reporting, but see the related discussions in Chapter 19.

In Illustration 7.1, a marketer and his customer agree to a forward selling price of $4.00 when the cost of the commodity was $3.40. At the same time, the forward-looking futures market allowed the marketer to purchase futures contracts at $3.45. When it came time to deliver the commodity, the cost of the physical commodity had risen by 35 cents. He purchased the physical for $3.75 and delivered it to his customer. (For simplicity, delivery costs have been disregarded.) Simultaneously, he sold a futures contract at $3.75 to offset the long contract he had established at $3.45 when he set his forward selling price. The 30-cent futures gain helps offset the 35-cent cost increase in the physical commodity. Values are based on one unit of the commodity.

Illustration 7.1

Hedging Fixed-Price Sale

	Physical Commodity	Hedge with Futures	Combined
Sale commitment date:			
Fixed selling price	$4.00		
Commodity price	$3.40	$3.45	
Intended margin	$0.60		
Delivery date:			
Commodity price	$3.75	$3.75	
Actual margin	$0.25	$0.30	$0.55
Effect of price change	-$0.35	$0.30	-$0.05
Recap:			
Intended margin			$0.60
Margin without hedge			$0.25
Margin with hedge			$0.55
Basis loss (see chapter 13)			$0.05

Futures were purchased at $3.45 and sold at $3.75, for a 30-cent gain

One challenge of the futures contract, especially for a marketer who sells in small quantities, is that the standard contract quantity may exceed customer commitments to the marketer. Even if it doesn't, most likely those commitments will not denominate in standard contract quantities, and you can't buy partial futures contracts.

In practice, the marketer will likely aggregate commitments from a variety of customers in order to obtain sufficient quantity to hedge, converting a straightforward hedging exercise into a record-keeping extravaganza—or nightmare, depending upon your persuasion! If the marketer does not have sufficient fixed-price business, hedging the price risk with standardized futures contracts can be difficult.

As a fourth option, the marketer can swap the price with an over-the-counter market maker. This technique has the advantage of allowing the marketer to customize the quantity to the actual size of his sales at risk. However, an over-the-counter market introduces a performance and credit risk that does not exist with a regulated exchange. See related discussions in Chapters 6 and 16.

Like most futures contracts, swaps settle financially, meaning that the physical product does not change hands. Rather, the parties to the swap contract exchange cash, flowing in the direction of the party that has benefited from the price movement. When using either futures contracts or swap contracts, the marketer must have some other method of obtaining the physical product, at market price, in order to meet delivery obligations.

Capped-Price Sales

In a capped-price contract, a marketer is offering a customer future delivery of product at the lower of the market price determined at delivery or the cap price established when the contract is executed. The actual price will depend upon where the market is trading when the product is delivered.

While the customer will still be protected from a price increase above the cap, **capped-price sales differ from fixed-price sales in that the customer will benefit from price declines.** The marketer has taken on a one-directional price risk.

If the price goes up, he must still deliver to the customer at the cap price. However, if the price declines, it is as if the capped-price contract did not exist. The customer will pay the market price.

If the marketer fixes his cost with a financial instrument to protect himself against price increases, just as he did in the previous fixed-price example (Illustration 7.1), he will lose money if the product cost declines before delivery. He will still report a normal margin when he delivers the physical product, but he will lose value on the futures contract or swap agreement that fixed the cost. He'd rather have had no such contract (at least when prices decline).

Illustration 7.2 demonstrates this. When the marketer and the customer agree to the cap price, the marketer purchases a futures contract at $3.45, mindful only of the potential effect of higher prices on his profit margin, as illustrated in the previous example. However, when the commodity price instead declines, he sells the futures contract at a loss of 70 cents. Even though he is able to purchase the physical commodity at the lower cost of $2.75, the selling price has also declined. He makes an acceptable margin on the physical sale, but he must eat the futures loss, with insufficient offsetting benefit from the sale of the physical commodity. Again, values are shown per unit of commodity.

The customer receives the best of both worlds: price protection and the benefit of price declines. However, without the ability to hedge with a futures or a swap contract, how does a marketer protect against the risk of the price increasing beyond the cap price before delivery, when he must supply his customer with more expensive product that will compromise his profit margin?

A marketer that conveys price caps to its customers has essentially granted them an option, whether or not they paid for it. If the market price goes above the cap price, the customer can exercise his option of taking delivery at the cap price. However, if the price declines, the customer does not need to exercise his option because he can purchase the product at the market price. In reality, the customer never really needs to exercise an option; he gets the cap price automatically if it applies. However, the concept shows how the marketer ought to evaluate his own risk.

To hedge his price risk, the marketer needs someone who will take on his one-directional price risk at an affordable cost, just as he did for his customers. Then, he can pass that cost through to his customers as they agree to the capped-price contract. After all, they shouldn't get something for nothing!

Illustration 7.2

Hedging Capped Sale with Futures

Prices Assumed to Increase, but Decrease Instead

	Physical Commodity	Hedge with Futures	Combined
Sale commitment date:			
Capped selling price	$4.15		
Commodity price	$3.40	$3.45	
Intended margin (at the cap)	$0.75		
Delivery date:			
Selling price	$3.25		
Commodity price	$2.75	$2.75	
Actual margin	$0.50	-$0.70	-$0.20
Effect of price change	-$0.25	-$0.70	-$0.95
Recap:			
Intended margin			$0.75
Margin without hedge			$0.50
Margin with hedge			-$0.20

Futures were purchased at $3.45 and sold at $2.75, for a 70-cent loss
Hedging a capped sale with futures loses money when prices decline!

He can find a third party to assume his risk in the futures market. He will be looking for someone to sell him an option to buy the commodity at a fixed price, a price that would render an acceptable margin on a sale at the cap price. Then, when the commodity price increases and the customer benefits at his expense, he'll recoup his own benefit from the futures market.

This type of option is a call option, which conveys to its holder the right, but not the obligation, to purchase an underlying commodity at a predetermined strike price. When the cost of this option is charged to the customer, the hedging cost is effectively eliminated, but for the administrative costs of running a hedge program. Since the customer is receiving the benefit of the option, it only seems appropriate he bear the cost. In practice, companies may opt to share this cost with their customers as part of an overall marketing plan aimed at customer retention and loyalty.

Depending upon the commodity and the quantity, one may need the customization offered by an over-the-counter market maker. Otherwise, the benefits of a regulated futures market apply, including liquidity, standardization, cash management, accounting, and minimizing credit risk.

In Illustration 7.3, when the marketer and his customer agreed to a cap price of $4.15, the marketer purchased a call option with a strike price of $3.75. This option would allow him to create a long futures position at $3.75, should the futures price exceed that at delivery. The cost of the option was 20 cents, which the marketer collected from his customer and then remitted to the exchange. At delivery, the futures price of $4.10 was indeed higher than the option strike price. The option produced 35 cents in income ($4.10 - $3.75), which helped restore the profit margin to the intended amount. Values are shown per unit of commodity.

Illustration 7.3

Hedging Capped Sale with Options

Prices Increase

	Physical Commodity	Hedge with Options	Combined
Sale commitment date:			
Capped selling price	$4.15		
Option strike price	$3.75	$3.75	
Option premium (charged to customer)	$0.20	-$0.20	$0.00
Intended margin	$0.60	-$0.20	$0.40
Delivery date:			
Selling price (capped)	$4.15		
Commodity price	$4.10	$4.10	
Option premium (above)	$0.20	-$0.20	$0.00
Actual margin	$0.25	$0.15	$0.40
Effect of price change	-$0.35	$0.35	$0.00
Recap:			
Intended margin			$0.40
Margin without hedge			$0.25
Margin with hedge			$0.40

Options were exercised, resulting in futures gains restoring margin
Futures acquired via option at $3.75 were sold at $4.10, for a 35-cent gain

Fixed with Downside

Another type of capped-price sales program arises when a marketer offers a fixed-price contract that also allows its customers to participate in price declines, the so-called fixed with downside price-protection program. This is essentially the same as the capped-price program described above, with the cap price set at the current forward-market price for the projected period of delivery rather than at a price that exceeds the current forward-market price. The option for this program costs more because the downside risk is imminent. There's no buffer between the current forward-market price and the cap price.

As an alternative to call options, the fixed with downside price-protection program can be hedged equivalently with futures contracts and put options with a strike price that allows for the expected margin. Whereas a call option allows its holder to buy a futures contract at its strike price, a put option will allow its holder to sell a futures contract at its strike price. These put options will allow the marketer to prevent any losses on the futures contracts in the event of declines in the commodity price, when the customer will likely be entitled to a price below the cap price (assuming that selling prices are moving in lockstep with the commodity cost).

Managing a hedge constructed with two instruments, a futures contract and a put option, adds complexity to executing the hedge because two separate contracts may need to be traded in fast-moving markets, at both hedge inception and hedge exit. **Since complexity can often translate into execution errors, reducing complexity in a hedge is generally a good idea.** In this instance, using only call options is simpler. However, if you can buy the put options and futures more economically than you can buy the equivalent call options, you may be able to justify the added complexity.

Complexities in Forward Programs

The profit margin expectations on capped-price programs differ from those on fixed-price programs, in that the margin on deliveries below the cap price is not fixed. It is market-driven. There is no guarantee that pre-delivery declines in cost and selling price will correlate. Your selling price may drop more than your cost. You already have this risk on other classes of trade that don't require hedges. Just make sure that you can recoup the cost of your options without expecting a larger margin to pay for them. You may not earn it.

Illustration 7.4 uses the same set of data as the previous example, except that the commodity price declines. When the physical cost hits $2.75, the option is not needed, and it expires worthless. But that's okay because the customer paid for it anyway. The marketer purchases the commodity at $2.75 and delivers it to the customer, receiving the same price that all customers in this class of trade pay him. The margin happens to grow because the cost has dropped more than the selling price has.

Illustration 7.4

Hedging Capped Sale with Options
Prices Decrease

	Physical Commodity	Hedge with Options	Combined
Sale commitment date:			
Capped selling price	$4.15		
Option strike price	$3.75	$3.75	
Option premium (charged to customer)	$0.20	-$0.20	$0.00
Intended margin	$0.60	-$0.20	$0.40
Delivery date:			
Selling price	$3.25		
Commodity price	$2.75		
Option premium (above)	$0.20	-$0.20	$0.00
Actual margin	$0.70	-$0.20	$0.50
Effect of price change before delivery	$0.10	$0.00	$0.10
Recap:			
Intended margin			$0.40
Margin without hedge			$0.70
Margin with hedge			$0.50

Options expired worthless
Margins better than expected as cost dropped more than selling price

As described in Chapter 4, each month's commodity price differs. In a fixed-price program, hedgers will average the cost of the months included in the hedge period. The months with larger quantities of the commodity at risk will be assigned commensurate weighting in calculating the average strip cost. Nevertheless, because the monthly costs vary and the fixed selling price does not, unit margins will vary each month.

This issue does not affect capped-price programs in the same way because the hedger has the discretion to choose the correct strike price across all months. What will vary, however, is the cost of those options in each month. Two factors will drive option cost higher. First, options for months that are further in the future will have a higher time value. Second, options for months with higher futures prices will be more expensive. The intended unit margin in months with higher option costs will be lower than in months when the option costs are lower, assuming deliveries occur at or above the cap price.

The risk associated with capped-price contracts usually cannot be hedged without the use of some financially settled instrument. Owning the physical commodity exposes the marketer to a market price that can float in either direction. To fix the price in one direction and not the other requires a derivative of the underlying commodity. The marketer can transfer the management of the hedge to a supplier, but can expect to pay a higher cost for this service.

If, under a capped-price program, the marketer looks to his supplier to fix the cost of his future purchases of the product, he'll need to secure downside price protection on those purchases. He'll have a very complex hedge structure—to price, to execute, and to account for—the reasons for which are beyond the scope of this book.

Because exchange-traded options denominate in the same quantities as the futures contracts that underlie them, hedgers face the same challenges pertaining to quantities on capped-price programs as they do on fixed-price programs.

Many over-the-counter options settle based upon the average of prices across an entire month. If a marketer uses such an option to hedge its capped-price program, there may be times when it will not protect the risk. For example, if the strike price of the call option is $3.50, and the commodity price averaged $3.50 for the entire month, the marketer will receive no compensation when the option settles. However, the $3.50 average may have included certain days when the commodity cost was $3.60, and other days when it was $3.40. On those days when the commodity cost was $3.60, commodity purchases compromised the margin. Exchange-traded options can be exercised (or sold) whenever needed, and would have worked as intended in this scenario, provided the hedger managed them properly.

Lastly, if a marketer does not fix the customer's quantity under either a fixed-price or a capped-price program, he has not eliminated all of the price risk. He'll need to estimate the quantity at risk to determine how much to hedge. Any differences between the quantities he hedges and the quantities he delivers under the program will become unhedged (or overhedged) risk. There is a cost to this risk. If a marketer can find some way to pass that risk on to the customer, or at least share it with the customer, he has mitigated some of that risk. See related discussion in Chapter 15.

CHAPTER 8

Consumables

When you lock in a commodity cost below your budgeted cost, you've increased your chances of having a good year.

Many manufacturers and producers use commodities to make their products. Other businesses, such as farming operations, fishing operations, airlines, and heavy industries, rely on energy commodities to bring their products or services to market. An escalation in the cost of these commodities will result in a higher cost of doing business and a higher cost of the product or service they sell.

You can't always pass the additional cost on to the consumer. Maybe there are alternatives to your product, or you have competitors who can better absorb the cost increases. Maybe you have concerned shareholders, or certain business benchmarks, such as bank debt covenants, that require you to manage your costs to a budget. Or maybe you've already fixed the selling price for your product or service, and any increase in your cost to produce it would eat into your margin and your bottom line.

If any of the above scenarios apply, it may be time to consider hedging the cost of the commodities used in your process. What types of consumables might we consider in this discussion? Electricity to run machinery and lighting, gasoline and diesel fuel to power vehicles and vessels, fertilizer to grow crops, copper that becomes part of an assembly, and jet fuel to power airplanes are good examples.

Illustration 8.1

Hedging Consumable

Prices Increase

	Hedge with Paper	Physical Commodity	Combined
Budget:			
Quantity	100,000	100,000	
Per-unit cost		$3.10	
Total budgeted cost		$310,000	
Actual:			
Purchase futures	$3.00		
Sell futures/purchase physical (months later)	$3.40	$3.40	
Increase in futures price	$0.40		
Gain on futures contracts	$40,000		
Total actual cost		$340,000	
Comparison to budget	$40,000	-$30,000	$10,000
Recap:			
Budgeted cost			$310,000
Cost without hedge			$340,000
Cost with hedge			$300,000

Actual quantity presumed the same as budgeted quantity

A business trying to hedge consumables might want a long futures position in the relevant commodity prior to the consumption period. The quantity should approximate the expected usage for that period. The long position effectively locks in the cost of consumption for that commodity. Once the cost is fixed, the hedger cannot realize the benefit of a price decline before he purchases the commodity itself. This concession represents the cost of eliminating the risk of price increases.

A common way to benchmark hedge performance on consumables is to compare the locked-in cost to a budget. If you can secure a cost not to exceed your budgeted cost, then you've increased the likelihood that you will achieve budgeted performance. Once the actual consumable has been purchased, or its cost has otherwise been established, the hedge should be liquidated. Theoretically, the gain or loss on the futures position should offset the difference between what you expected to pay and what you did pay for the consumable.

In Illustration 8.1, a company benchmarks its cost against a budget of $3.10, and then hedges the exposure before the period of consumption when it sees a lower futures price of $3.00. When the consumption period arrives, the commodity cost has risen to $3.40. Simultaneous with the purchase of the physical commodity at $3.40, the company sells a futures contract at $3.40, producing a futures gain of 40 cents ($3.40 - $3.00). This gain lowers the effective cost to $3.00.

The above example worked as intended. When the cost of the commodity increased before the period of consumption, the company was able to maintain a cost below its budgeted cost when it realized a gain on the futures contracts. I simplified the model to illustrate the hedging theory. In practice, the actual quantity would most likely vary from the budgeted quantity. Furthermore, the purchase cost of the physical commodity would most likely differ from the selling price of the futures contract. I've included a more thorough example in Chapter 13 to address this basis issue. There are also challenges in the timing of a hedge like this, which I'll address soon under "Why Settlement Matters."

Sometimes, you give up a benefit when you hedge. In Illustration 8.2, you see the same fact pattern as shown in the previous example, except the price of the commodity goes down. Although the company could have purchased the commodity at lower overall cost had it not hedged, it nevertheless achieved its hedging objective: purchasing the commodity below budget.

Illustration 8.2

Hedging Consumable

Prices Decrease

	Hedge with Paper	Physical Commodity	Combined
Budget:			
Quantity	100,000	100,000	
Per-unit cost		$3.10	
Total budgeted cost		$310,000	
Actual:			
Purchase futures	$3.00		
Sell futures/purchase physical (months later)	$2.75	$2.75	
Decrease in futures price	-$0.25		
Loss on futures contracts	-$25,000		
Total actual cost		$275,000	
Comparison to budget	-$25,000	$35,000	$10,000
Recap:			
Budgeted cost			$310,000
Cost without hedge			$275,000
Cost with hedge			$300,000

Actual quantity presumed the same as budgeted quantity

Scale can be an issue when hedging consumables. You need enough quantity for an entire monthly contract in order to hedge these commodities effectively with standard contracts. Some commodities trade in "mini" contract sizes. You may need to pool your demand with that of other similar businesses in order to execute a hedge. There are brokers who will seek to aggregate this demand for you.

Why Settlement Matters

There are two types of price settlement: (1) daily settlement, which is used to determine daily gains and losses on open positions and their effect on collateral requirements and interim financial statements; and (2) what I'll call ultimate settlement, which establishes the price at which you exit a contract. I address the latter type of settlement in the following paragraphs.

When you compare the exit price to the price at which you entered the contract, you determine your gain or loss on that contract. Comparing that gain or loss to the gain or loss on the business transaction that you were hedging will determine the adequacy of your hedge. Theoretically speaking, **the sum of all those gains and losses in a hedge with perfect price correlation should be zero.**

It may be best to hedge exposures on consumables with contracts that settle based on an average across the month rather than at one point in time. A contract that settles at one point in time may not represent the price that prevailed across the entire period.

Some contracts settle at the end of a month, or you can trade them to settle your position before they expire. Most over-the-counter swaps will settle based upon an average of the daily settlement prices over the period to which they pertain (usually one month). Using these average-price swaps will allow you to better match the cost associated with a production process that occurs consistently across the swap period.

To illustrate this point, suppose a gasoline contract traded at $3.00 per gallon for the first half of the month because a hurricane had just shut down some refineries. The hedger bought the contract five months ago at a price of $2.40. It's a good thing he had the contract, right? Well, it depends.

As the refineries came back online near the end of the month, the price dropped to $2.25 per gallon. While the average price for the month was roughly $2.75, his futures contract traded 50 cents lower near expiration, to his detriment, when he liquidated his long position. During the month, the business purchased gasoline at an average cost of $2.75 per gallon. The business expected to pay $2.40 based upon the entry price of the futures contract, yet the sale of the contract at the end of the month brought only $2.25. That's a bad result because there is no business benefit to offset the 15-cent loss on the futures contract ($2.25 selling price less $2.40 purchase price). Furthermore, the business ended up paying another 35 cents higher than its anticipated cost of $2.40.

Obviously, the opposite pricing scenario (when the price rises near the end of the period) would have resulted in a favorable hedging result. However, the intent of hedging is to reduce price risk by matching the cost and quantities with the period of consumption. A swap settling on average prices would have been a more appropriate hedging choice. The hedger would have collected 35 cents ($2.75 settlement based on average price less the $2.40 entry price) on the swap contract. These hedging proceeds would have reduced his effective cost to $2.40 ($2.75 paid less 35-cent hedging proceeds), which accomplishes the original intent.

Illustration 8.3 demonstrates the comparison of hedging with a swap or a futures contract, as described above. The two hedging columns represent two independent hedging choices. Each is then compared to the physical commodity column on the row labeled "Net hedging results."

Some swaps cannot be traded before they settle. What if you find out later that you chose the wrong period when you entered into your hedge? Maybe your production schedule accelerated and your July contract should really have been a June contract. If you need to liquidate such a swap early, you'll need to enter into another swap to lock the gain or loss on the first swap and to eliminate the remaining exposure in the first swap. It sounds complicated, but a good broker should be able to work through the required math for you.

This trade may come with some financial cost (or benefit), but the economics can be much more punitive if you simply carry the swap until it settles. Once the risk in the physical market resolves, you are carrying a swap without a counterbalancing physical position. There's nothing left to offset any change in the swap value. Furthermore, you haven't closed the hedge and locked in the appropriate gain or loss for the hedge

Illustration 8.3

Hedging Consumable
Why Settlement Matters

	Hedge with Avg-Price Swaps	Hedge with Futures	Physical Commodity
Budget:			
Quantity	100,000	100,000	100,000
Per-unit cost			$2.40
Total budgeted cost			$240,000
Actual:			
Purchase instruments	$2.40	$2.40	
Settle instruments & purchase physical (months later)	$2.75	$2.25	$2.75
Change in price	$0.35	-$0.15	
Results on instruments	$35,000	-$15,000	
Total actual cost			$275,000
Implied gain or loss	$35,000	-$15,000	-$35,000
Net hedging results	$0	-$50,000	

Actual quantity presumed the same as budgeted quantity
Budget premised on purchase price of hedging instrument

period that has elapsed. You now hold an absolute price risk on the remainder of the swap, and you have not offset the business gain or loss on the purchase of the commodity itself. **Hedges need to be closed when the risk that gave rise to them disappears. Otherwise, they exacerbate risk rather than reduce it.**

Best of Both Worlds

As described above, a long position on a consumable commodity locks in a cost. The hedger then loses any benefit of price declines. What if you want to retain the benefit of price declines, but you still need to protect against a substantial price increase? You want the best of both worlds! But, of course, you realize that nothing in life—or certainly in business—is free. What you want is an option, more specifically, a long call option. And the value of this option, its premium, is the price you will pay for the privilege you are seeking.

As already discussed, an option gives you the right, but not the obligation, to establish a position in a commodity contract at a predetermined price. A long call will give you the right to establish a long futures (or swap) position in a commodity contract. (There are OTC market makers who will sell an option on a swap.) If managed correctly, and absent other basis issues (discussed further in Chapter 13), this option will act like an insurance policy. You won't pay higher than the predetermined price for your commodity. You must, however, be willing to part with a premium today to secure that peace of mind.

Let's say the cost of electricity today is seven cents per kilowatt-hour (kWh). The swap market is offering eight cents per kWh six months forward. If the per-kWh price goes above ten cents, achieving budget will be very difficult. Your manufacturing process is highly dependent upon electricity. You could either execute the swap to lock in an eight-cent cost today, or cap the cost at ten cents by purchasing an option. The market wants one cent for that option. You think prices are going to stay the same or go lower, but you can't tolerate the risk of a cataclysmic event spiking the cost higher. You decide to purchase the call option for a penny.

If, in six months, the per-kWh cost is lower than ten cents, you pay the actual cost, and your option expires worthless. You lost the penny you paid for the option, but that was really an insurance premium against higher costs that never materialized. You're okay with that. If the per-kWh cost is less than seven cents, you'll have made out better than if you had swapped the cost out at eight cents six months ago.

Illustration 8.4

Hedging Consumable

Swap Versus Option

	Hedge with Avg-Price Swap	Hedge with Option: Price Up	Hedge with Option: Price Down
Option cost		$0.01	$0.01
Enter swap	$0.08	$0.10	
Settle swap	$0.12	$0.12	
Results on instruments	$0.04	$0.01	-$0.01
Budgeted per-unit cost	$0.10	$0.10	$0.10
Purchase physical	$0.12	$0.12	$0.06
Cost compared to budget	-$0.02	-$0.02	$0.04
Net hedging results	$0.02	-$0.01	$0.03

Option with strike price of $0.10 is premised on a swap
Swap is settled when physical is purchased, at presumably same price
Swap net hedging results will not vary with price direction

If the price exceeds ten cents, you will exercise your option and establish a long swap position at ten cents. You'll recoup any excess over ten cents, effectively capping your cost at ten cents (plus the penny you paid for the option). In hindsight, you'd rather have executed the swap at eight cents, since that is lower than the eleven-cent cost you incurred. But at least you still have a chance to make budget. Hindsight, as they say, is 20-20.

Illustration 8.4 shows three separate hedging scenarios for the same price risk, comparing the effect of hedging with swaps or options as described above. Since the results of hedging with options vary depending upon the price direction, the last two columns demonstrate each price-direction scenario. The actual price for the hedge period was twelve cents per kWh for the first two scenarios and six cents per kWh for the third scenario.

CHAPTER 9

Inventory

Inventory is always looking for the exit. Don't let it slip
through your hands before its time.

Inventory. It's what you as a businessperson sell and profit from. If it loses value, so do you. **If a business owns and holds a commodity, that business is in danger of losing value.** Commodity prices tend to have a mind of their own. They can fluctuate wildly. Let's consider some examples of ways to protect the value of the asset that is itching to drop to your bottom line—one way or the other: inventory.

Gold Miner

The leaders of a gold-mining company are doing some strategic planning. They want to understand the value of their business better. More importantly, they want to know how to protect the value. The company's most significant asset is its one gold mine. Engineers have provided an estimate of the amount of gold in the mine. Since the futures market provides price discovery, the company's top brass first looks at the market value of the gold in the mine and then reduces that by the estimated cost to extract it and to refine it. They soon realize there is ample value.

They also realize that the market value of gold, like any other commodity, changes daily, if not by the minute. Worldwide events and investor sentiment can send the value in either direction without notice. If the price of gold declines by $100 an ounce, the company will have lost $100 per ounce of value in its mine—and in its business. How can the company protect itself from such a decline in value?

Their company adds value by extracting and refining. A significant enough decline in the value of the commodity it owns can eliminate what value the company can add, rendering its business worthless. If it takes $1,000 an ounce to process the gold, and the price of gold drops below $1,000 an ounce, what's the sense in processing the gold? The costs of extracting and refining aren't going to fluctuate significantly. Although the company may discover methods that are more efficient, those processes and their associated costs have been honed over time. They won't change materially in the near future.

The commodity cost, however, most likely will change materially. After all, it is a commodity. Only the direction of the price is unknown. Given the current price for gold and the company's plans to sell its business sometime in the next few years, the leaders decide that they must find a way to manage the risk of a decline in price.

If the business were to sell gold futures at current futures prices, the price risk would be virtually eliminated. The company would protect the value of its business by protecting the value of its gold. It would want to sell futures contracts in the particular months when it expects to deliver the gold. As long as the grade of the refined gold matches the specifications of the futures contract, and the quantity of the physical gold approximates how many ounces the company sells in the futures market, it can manage its commodity price risk.

Gasoline Distributor

Here's another case study that should help clarify the economics. For $3.00 a gallon, a gasoline distributor purchases a boatload of gasoline. He will store it at his terminal until next month, when he anticipates selling it in its entirety.

As a distributor, he adds value to the commodity by managing its flow into the marketplace. His customers, who don't have sufficient storage capacity, purchasing power, or capital capacity, will compensate him for the service he provides. However, until they do, he runs the risk of losing value on the inventory, should the commodity cost decline. Given the modest per-gallon profit he makes from his customers, his profit could evaporate with just one day's price decline.

When he purchased the gasoline, the distributor entered into a hedge to protect its value by selling the appropriate month's futures contracts in the same quantity as his purchase, coincidentally at $3.00 a gallon. (In practice, the market will trade the futures at a price somewhat different from the current price for the physical product, but usually approximate to it.)

On the day after his purchase, a news event triggers a 25-cent plunge in the price of gasoline. Naturally, he drops his selling price to his customers by 25 cents, too, in order to stay in line with his competitors' prices. It's a good thing he hedged his product.

Illustration 9.1

Hedging Inventory

	Physical Commodity	Hedge with Futures	Combined
Quantity	11,000,000	-11,000,000	0
Price at inception	$3.00	$3.00	
Price at delivery	$2.75	$2.75	
Change in price	-$0.25	-$0.25	$0.00
Gain or loss in value	-$2,750,000	$2,750,000	$0

During the next month, he liquidates the inventory while the cost of gasoline remains at about $2.75. As he liquidates the inventory, he removes the hedge by purchasing gasoline futures contracts at an approximate price of $2.75. He has to write down his inventory by 25 cents, but he recoups this loss when he liquidates his futures position. Therefore, he realizes no gain or loss on the entire transaction, but for the profit margin he typically receives as a distributor when he sells gasoline to his customers. Had he not hedged this transaction, he would have realized a 25-cent loss while holding the inventory, which would have more than negated the profit he made when selling the product.

Illustration 9.1 demonstrates the example that I've just described. In hedging parlance, the distributor was "long the physical inventory" and "short the futures." Notice that a decline in the futures price of a short position renders a futures gain because the selling price is higher than the purchase price.

Opportunity Knocks

Sometimes, the futures market will reward you just for being in the business. Sometimes, it will penalize you. You'll want to exercise enough foresight to recognize when it's time to seize an opportunity—or run for the hills.

The futures market provides you this foresight. You don't need your own crystal ball. The futures market provides plenty of price discovery. It is a real marketplace where buyers and sellers transact real trades. **Those who buy and sell in future months do not know where the price will be when those months arrive, but collectively, they do establish what those prices are today. And that's valuable, because you can make business decisions based on those prices.** You can execute trades in those futures months yourself, to manage risk, to protect your own business interests, and, sometimes, to pick a ripe cherry off the tree of opportunity that awaits those who are watchful and ready. The key is to watch "the curve."

Remember the curve? It's the graph depicting monthly prices of the same commodity. We discussed it in Chapter 4.

If you hold inventory, a curve rising from left to right bears glad tidings, while a curve falling from left to right portends a difficult hedging environment. Why? Because moving to the right on the graph takes you further into the future. You'd certainly prefer to sell something in the future for a higher price than it costs you today, and you'd rather not sell something in the future for a lower price than it costs you today. It's that simple. For the hedging purists out there, a favorable futures curve, one that climbs from left to right, depicts a contango market; a curve that declines from left to right portrays a backwardated market.

The leftmost plot point on the futures curve will most likely approximate the price of the physical commodity because, with time to delivery short, uncertainty, and therefore risk, is more limited. There is a shorter timeframe for market-moving events to occur. The supply-and-demand factors that help establish the current market price of the physical product are discoverable today. Most market participants already know what they are. However, the further one projects into the future, the more difficult it is to anticipate the supply-and-demand factors that will help determine the price of a commodity, and the more likely it is that unpredictable events will occur. **With increased time comes more risk.** And the risk could move the price in either direction.

Can you see the opportunity in Illustration 9.2? The market is willing to pay more in the future for wheat than what it is worth today. That should get your attention!

Illustration 9.2

Wheat Futures Curve
Per Bushel Price as of 12/26/13

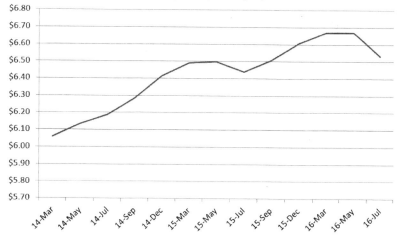

Do you remember the ripened cherry allusion? If you own a commodity today that has not been committed to a customer at a fixed price, and you can sell it forward on the futures market and hold it uncommitted (as to price) until the month of delivery, you might just be locking in a substantial gain. You will usually realize a sizeable portion of the gain shown on today's graph because the month for which you sell the futures contract will eventually become the first (or "prompt") futures month. And remember the above discussion about how the first plot point on the graph will approximate the cost of the physical commodity? If you patiently wait for the futures to "mature," you will realize most of the gain an overwhelming percentage of the time.

It gets even better. Don't forget, you need to protect your price risk on that uncommitted inventory anyway. **With the buy-hedge-and-hold strategy, not only will you realize a gain as the delivery month approaches and the difference between the futures price in the delivery month and the price for the physical commodity vanishes, but you will also be protecting the value of your inventory.** It sounds too good to be true. Yet it is true!

What's the catch? There will be times when the futures curve will not work in your favor, when the market is backwardated. It's then when the market will penalize you for being in the business. **When you hedge inventory in a backwardated market, you are selling it below cost.** That's when you might rather choose to minimize your inventory levels so you have little inventory price risk to hedge. And although selling below cost may sound like a bad idea, it may just beat the alternative of having unlimited price risk on your entire inventory! Would you rather lose a couple of cents on every gallon, pound, or ounce, or risk losing twenty-five cents on each by not hedging? Sometimes, hedgers face tough decisions.

To illustrate the benefits of the buy-hedge-and-hold strategy, let's reconsider the prior example. With ample product to meet customer needs for several months, our distributor has some flexibility. Instead of liquidating the boatload of inventory in the following month, suppose he chooses to carry the inventory for six months because the futures price six months forward is trading 15 cents higher than that of the front month. So, instead of selling the gasoline into the futures market at $3.00 per gallon, he sells it at $3.15.

Let's assume that the price of physical gasoline holds at $2.75 for six months. At delivery, the futures contract is trading much closer to the physical price. So, the 15-cent commodity price difference at hedge inception has collapsed. The distributor purchases a futures contract at approximately the same $2.75 price as the physical product is selling for in order to cancel the hedge. He realizes a futures gain of 40 cents ($3.15 minus $2.75) instead of 25 cents, as in the previous example. Including the 25-cent inventory write-down, the distributor walks away with a 15-cent gain, plus the margin he will earn when he delivers the product to his customers. It sure pays to be in the gasoline business, at least on this day.

Illustration 9.3 summarizes the example.

Illustration 9.3
Making Money Hedging Inventory

	Physical Commodity	Hedge with Futures	Combined
Quantity	11,000,000	-11,000,000	0
Price at inception	$3.00	$3.15	
Price at delivery	$2.75	$2.75	
Change in price	-$0.25	-$0.40	$0.15
Gain or loss in value	-$2,750,000	$4,400,000	$1,650,000

Always remember that it costs money to carry inventory. Those costs should be considered when evaluating buy-hedge-and-hold strategies. You may also be in for a wild ride in the accounting books before you land on statements with a longer time horizon and higher profits. (See accounting discussion in Chapter 19.) Yet, for companies with discretionary storage and a low cost of capital, contango markets can offer handsome rewards.

Getting Creative

When a favorable futures curve presents an opportunity to sell forward and lock in a gain, you might wish you had more inventory to sell. That's when it's time for some creative thought. Although some might consider such strategies speculative, they do not constitute price speculation on futures contracts because you'll have an offsetting physical position.

First, realize that it takes money to make money. If you have access to cash, or if you can demonstrate the value of your strategy to a willing lender, you can take advantage of favorable pricing in the futures market.

You also need to understand the hedging strategy and know how to manage it, which takes a certain level of business sophistication. Perhaps you are developing more of that than your peers down the street currently possess.

Maybe, just maybe, some of your competitors have some inventory, or storage, with which they are willing to part. Maybe they are short on cash and can't afford to hold inventory to earn the substantial hedging gain the futures market is offering them. They may need those dollars simply to meet payroll. Or maybe they already have too much debt, and their lenders won't allow them to participate. Maybe they simply don't understand how the futures market works, or can't be bothered.

You may have an opportunity to purchase their product, right where it is, hedge it, hold it until you realize your gain, and then sell it back to them at a market price. Or, perhaps they will rent you their storage. You could purchase the commodity elsewhere, transport it to the storage facility, hedge and hold it, and then liquidate it into the cash market once you've realized your hedging gains.

When considering hedging strategies that go beyond your normal business operation, always consider how much capital you will need to deploy and how much you expect to earn on your investment. This analysis should factor in all relevant costs, including the time needed to manage the strategy to its completion.

Whenever you invest money in any business endeavor, always understand the return you expect to earn. Cash has unlimited investment potential. You can deploy it in the manner described above, or you can purchase stock, bonds, or other liquid investments, or buy another business. Yet, because you are already in a business that deals with a certain commodity, you may have an opportunity not available to others. Always make sure that investment is more beneficial than others you could make.

Creative thinking should not be limited to contango markets. **If you hold inventory in a backwardated market, you'll prevent hedging losses if you can liquidate your inventory more quickly than usual.** You'll not want to do this at the expense of creating your own supply shortage, with its related problems and cost. Nor will you want to incur more logistical costs to accelerate the inventory reduction than the hedging losses you may prevent. Nevertheless, it will certainly be beneficial to consider alternatives to reducing your risk. A thoughtful and balanced cost/benefit analysis will shed light on the best decision.

Words of Caution

Always be aware of the counterparty's credit standing. If you purchase their product and hedge it, will you have control over it? Or, will they sell your product, collect cash from customers, and then default on their obligation to repurchase the commodity from you? You may want to consult with a lawyer to secure your interest in the inventory. Often, however, the first step would be to assess the creditworthiness of your business partner.

What are the physical properties of the product you are purchasing and hedging? Is there a risk of spoilage, or lack of yield? **Hedging a product that will not bring full value at maturity is tantamount to taking an open-ended price risk in the futures market.** You'd potentially be worse off than if you did nothing. If you can insure the value of the inventory, however, you may not need to worry about this.

What are the controls on the inventory? Is there a risk of loss due to theft? And who owns that risk? Again, insurance may remedy this pitfall.

Finally, you'll need an exit strategy. You'll need to liquidate the physical commodity before expiration of the futures contracts, but also far enough in the future to earn the intended gain. You may already be in a business that will allow you to manage a timely liquidation, or you may need to hire another party to help. You don't want to be stuck with a longer-term hedging exercise, when changes in the futures curve may jeopardize the profits of your original strategy.

CHAPTER 10

Interest Cost

Commodity price risk sometimes lurks where you least expect it.

When you think about the term *commodity price risk*, you may begin to question why I've included a chapter entitled "Interest Cost." However, upon further examination, you will see that debt that creates interest cost meets our definition of a commodity, for debt is a staple in running certain businesses, and its interest rates can fluctuate. Interest cost is subject to the whims of the marketplace just as other commodity costs are, when global supply-and-demand imbalances challenge the profitability of unsuspecting and far-removed businesses.

All businesses need money, or so-called capital, to operate. Debt is one typical source of capital, and its risk can be hedged. Let's start with some background on how businesses attract and pay for the capital they use, which will shed more light on why it is important to hedge interest cost.

Forms of Business Capital

There are two ways to fund a business enterprise. One is exclusively from its owners. It comes in the form of owner contributions to the business's capital, and cash generated by the business and retained in the business for future use. In a corporate setting, this source of funding is referred to as shareholders' equity. Its cost is the financial reward that its owners expect in return for the risk they are assuming by investing in the business. That reward can come in the form of dividends paid out of the cash generated by the business, or growth in the value of the enterprise. Often, it comes in both forms.

Owner capital can have its limitations, especially for companies that are not publicly traded. Often, owners of private companies have much of their wealth already tied up in the business. They may be unwilling or unable to put additional personal dollars at risk. In order to grow a business, or in some cases to maintain one, most businesses will need to seek outside capital. Let's face it. You need money to make money.

Enter the second form of financing a business: cash (or other assets) from third-party lenders. You can think of this class of capital as debt capital. Common third-party lenders include banks, equipment leasing companies, sellers of certain assets (e.g., vehicles or real estate), bondholders, and other organizations whose sole business is to lend money. Bond-holders can run the gamut of investors, from individuals to pension plans, who like a steady flow of income and who like to be paid before shareholders are. The cost of debt capital is interest expense, which varies with each specific arrangement. A legal loan document will spell out the terms of debt and, therein, one can learn the true cost of the debt.

Typically, debt capital is less expensive than owner capital. Debtors are legally bound to pay maturing debt principal and interest before paying dividends to the business's owners. Because they receive higher priority in the cash payout queue, lenders are willing to accept a lower return. They hold less risk than the business's owners do. Furthermore, interest expense is tax deductible, whereas dividends are not. Nevertheless, interest expense can be a very significant component factoring into the computation of net income. If the interest cost is unmanageably high, businesses may struggle to thrive, if not survive.

From a risk standpoint, the cost of owner capital is not a concern. Dividends are simply a transfer of the same owners' wealth from inside the company to outside of it. If you move coins from your left pants pocket to your right pants pocket, they are in a different location but you still have them. However, **the cost of debt capital reduces owner wealth. You're** transferring money to a third party. That's why it is a business risk to hedge.

Debt Terms

Attaining a basic understanding of how debt capital works is important to understanding how to hedge its cost. Any loan agreement between a borrower and a lender will specify certain terms associated with a borrowing. Those terms typically include the amount of the borrowing (principal), the duration of the borrowing (term), the rate at which it will be paid down (amortization), the periodic amount to be paid and when (payments), the interest cost and how it is computed (interest rate), and any arrangement that protects the lender's financial investment in the borrower (e.g., security).

Debt is often tied to a business's assets. Those assets may have been acquired with the funds from the borrowing or they may pre-date the borrowing. The borrower may pledge those assets as collateral (security) to the lender in exchange for more favorable lending terms, or simply for access to the debt capital itself. How the debt is to be repaid will be spelled out up front by the loan agreement. Usually, the borrower will make monthly payments to the lender, and the term of the debt will not exceed the expected life of the pledged assets.

A borrower who defaults on a loan (e.g., by failing to make timely payments) runs the risk of having the pledged assets seized by the lender. The lender does not really want this outcome. He'd rather have the cash, and he doesn't want to impair the business's ability to generate additional cash to pay off the debt. Typically, a monitoring process ensues to make sure the borrower can honor his obligation. Other side agreements may enter the picture to shore up the lender's investment.

Often, a portion of the monthly payments will reduce the balance of money owed (debt principal). The remainder of each payment represents the interest cost associated with carrying the remaining debt balance. The faster the principal is paid off (retired), the lower the interest expense incurred.

The rate at which a debt is reduced is referred to as debt principal amortization, or simply amortization for short. The amount of the monthly payments can be fixed or variable, depending upon the terms of the specific loan agreement. Regardless, the interest can be computed with exactitude, as governed by the loan agreement. **Because interest expense is determined by formula, it is conducive to hedging instruments,** the terms of which can be mated to the formula much like color-coded wires are attached for an EKG.

The lender assumes a risk by lending cash to an entity whose future cash flows are uncertain. That lender may be competing with other lenders for the same cash flow dollars of the business. Prospective borrowers can foster a competitive landscape for prospective lenders by exercising a healthy portion of due diligence, and they are well advised to do so.

Lenders, on the other hand, will seek some portion of control to protect their own business interests. Ultimately, lenders are interested in borrowers whose businesses promise a strong cash flow to support repayment of debt. Yet it is much easier to bind the assets that generate the cash flow than it is to bind the cash flow itself.

Such are the elements that factor into debt negotiations. Perhaps the more significant factor, however, will be to agree on how the interest cost will be calculated.

How Interest Is Assessed on Debt

Some loan agreements are negotiated with fixed interest rates, some with variable rates. Variable interest rates are usually determined by adding a fixed, agreed-upon adjustment (an adder) to an agreed-upon index, like the prime interest rate. The index will vary with market conditions, and that variable component causes the negotiated interest rate to vary with the market.

For example, a loan agreement might define a variable interest rate as prime plus three (sometimes referred to as three hundred basis points). If prime is 4 percent, then interest will be computed using an interest rate of 7 percent. When the prime rate changes, so does the interest rate used in the calculation.

LIBOR is another common index used in calculating variable rates on loans. The agreed-upon index is typically one with which peer companies might conduct business. Using a common index provides a relevant context for assessing interest.

It will also allow for a myriad of hedging partners. For more on LIBOR, see http://en.wikipedia.org/wiki/Libor.

The periodic interest cost on a loan is computed by multiplying the interest rate for the period by the remaining principal balance as of the beginning of the period. When interest rates increase, variable-rate debt becomes more expensive. When interest rates decline, interest on variable-rate debt also declines. Once a rate is fixed, the interest rate environment has no effect on the interest expense applicable to that particular fixed-rate debt.

There is an important caveat to this rule. When a large principal payment is due as the last scheduled payment on the amortization schedule of a fixed-rate loan, such a "balloon payment" is usually refinanced under another loan agreement. The interest cost under a new loan agreement will certainly be influenced by market interest rates when the loan is negotiated, even though its principal originated from a fixed-rate loan.

Whether a loan agreement is to contain a fixed or variable interest cost is a key negotiating point. Once the parties have agreed whether to fix the interest cost, the rate itself is still subject to negotiation. With a fixed-rate agreement, the negotiation relates to establishing the absolute rate to be used to calculate the interest cost; with a variable-rate agreement, the negotiation pertains to determining the adder and the index to be used in computing the periodic interest.

Hedging Interest Cost

Some businesses are more susceptible to changes in interest rates than are others. For example, financing companies who extend short-term loans or write short-term equipment leases have some ability to pass through the higher costs associated with interest-rate increases on their own variable-rate debt. On the other hand, real estate companies, or automobile dealers who provide financing, typically are exposed to increases in interest rates over a longer term, as the duration of their leases or loans receivable determines.

Any business that is able to peg its revenue stream with fluctuations in interest rates may already have a hedge on its profitability. All other businesses with significant

variable-rate debt loads are at risk for rising interest rates. As with all forms of hedging, those businesses that are more susceptible to cost increases need to assess the risk.

By far, **the most important time to contain interest cost is up front, before you execute the original loan document.** If you are in a position of negotiating strength, a competitive process will help to minimize your cost and land you with a more favorable lending partner and loan agreement. However, hedging interest cost need not end once you finalize the up-front negotiation.

There are several methods of hedging interest costs on existing debt, which usually convert all or a portion of the debt's interest cost from variable to fixed. One of the more common tools is an interest-rate swap.

An interest-rate swap is a contract that derives its value from the comparison of two interest rates. When converting from a variable to a fixed rate, or vice versa, one of the legs of the swap will be a fixed interest rate, while the other will be an average of a variable interest-rate index over the term of the swap. The variable leg of the swap opposes the variable rate in the debt, effectively eliminating the variable rate in favor of the fixed-rate leg of the swap.

If you are trying to hedge against interest-rate increases, ideally you will look for a swap with the same index used to calculate the interest on the debt you are hedging. For example, if your debt's interest is calculated based upon LIBOR plus two, you will want to find a LIBOR-based swap. You will also want to match the remaining term in the debt with the term of the swap, unless, of course, you don't perceive the same level of risk throughout the remaining term of the debt. Choosing to fix the interest rate over only a certain portion of the remaining debt term is still feasible. Because of the complexities involved, check with several market makers to make sure that the quoted price optimizes your risk-avoidance goal.

Where do you find such a swap? Your first stop may be the lender. The lender should best understand the rate structure in the debt, since he is already a party to it. However, he may not trade interest-rate swaps, or he may not price one competitively with the market.

It matters not whether you trade the swap with the lender or with some other party. The swap stands apart from the debt, but when taken together serves to fix the rate and eliminate the risk associated with the debt's variable rate. You just might find a better price with someone other than your lender. Moreover, **if your debt's variable interest rate is premised on a common index, you can find plenty of parties to quote the swap, each with a different perception of its value and a different appetite to trade it.**

You will incur more cost in the near term when you fix the interest rate on variable-rate debt. For example, if your variable rate calculates to 5 percent, the fixed rate that results from a swap will be higher, perhaps 7 percent. Whoever takes the other side of your swap is moving from a fixed rate, with its relatively lower risk profile, to a higher-risk variable rate. There's a cost to this risk transfer, and your counterparty needs to be compensated for assuming the risk that you no longer want. Whether you incur more cost in the long term is anyone's guess. Such is the nature of hedging interest cost.

Generally, because risk increases with uncertainty, and because there is more uncertainty when the time horizon is longer, the additional cost you incur when converting to a fixed rate will be higher on debt that has a longer remaining term. From time to time, however, unusual interest-rate market conditions may suggest otherwise.

When you fix the rate on a variable-rate loan, you are also forgoing any of the benefit, should the index rate used in calculating your interest cost decline. Yet again, you don't get something for nothing! You're exchanging risk for certainty.

There may be times when you hold fixed-rate debt but you would prefer a variable rate. Trading the swap described above in the opposite direction will accomplish this. Your interest rate will track with whatever index forms the variable leg in the swap. If the fixed rate on your debt is higher than the market's fixed rate for debt of comparable term, you will incur the additional cost over the remaining term even if you convert to a variable rate.

Another method of hedging interest cost is to negotiate a clause in the original loan document that will allow you to convert the interest rate from variable to fixed (or vice versa) at any point over the term of the loan. For some companies, this method can simplify the accounting ramifications of interest-rate swaps. (See also the discussion to come regarding accounting considerations.) It may also eliminate the need to negotiate a swap agreement with another party later.

In addition to the challenges and time associated with negotiating another swap agreement, that party's agreement may require margin calls on declines in the swap's value, whereas the lender's embedded swap likely will not. However, be wary of any hidden costs when embedding an elective swap in the original loan document. If your original loan negotiation was competitive, you will likely discover any hidden costs associated with this privilege.

Best of Both Worlds

What if you hold variable-rate debt and your business can no longer tolerate the risk of rate increases, but you don't want to walk away from a low-interest-rate environment—or the likelihood that rates could decline further? You're really only looking for insurance against a catastrophic rise in interest rates.

An interest-rate cap will provide this measure of protection. It works much like a call option on a commodity, where you can exercise the option at its strike price if the price of the underlying commodity rises above that price.

Let's say your variable-rate debt has a current interest rate of 5 percent. You've looked at swaps, but the market is pricing them at about 7 percent, and you think that's too high. You like paying the lower rate. You just want some protection in case the market gets out of hand.

You've run amortization schedules at various interest rates, and you've found that the interest costs at rates above 9 percent would be too much for your business's cash flow to bear. So, you decide to ask for quotes for a cap at 9 percent. You'll evaluate the best quote to make sure that the premium is reasonable for the protection you are buying. Once you agree to terms, you'll still enjoy the market's lower interest rates. You judge the peace of mind to be worth the cost.

With an interest-rate cap, you essentially limit your exposure to interest-rate increases up to the cap rate. You pay an up-front premium to the counterparty for this privilege. With a cap, you can choose a duration that coincides with the remaining term of the debt you are hedging, you can choose to cap only the exposure beyond the near-term time horizon, or you can select a shorter term and reassess the risk later, since the lower future principal comes with less exposure anyway.

You may have come to realize that the alternatives are limitless. These days, computer models can price just about any scenario into a swap or a cap. If you keep your swaps and caps straightforward and use a standard index, you'll be better able to liquidate them early at reasonable values, should you so desire, since more market makers will be willing to quote them.

Early Exit

Unlike many of the futures, options, and swaps that we've considered thus far, interest-rate derivatives tend to be long term in nature because they're tied to debt that often spans years. You should consider the long-term implications of these instruments before executing them.

It may cost you money to exit interest-rate swaps early, if you need to. Will you be selling your business, or the particular property that secures the underlying debt? And might you want to convert back to a variable (or fixed) interest rate? You'll want to understand the potential cost up front.

The best hedge you can make on interest cost is to have none of it. Yet that denies the less-costly attributes of debt capital versus owners' capital. Should you retire your debt early, you may be left with an unopposed interest-rate swap, which presents risk. The swap contains a forward-pricing component, and possibly even a penalty provision, that may make it costly to terminate. Nonetheless, terminate it you should...or at least nullify its effect. An alternative to a costly termination is to invert the impact with another swap traded elsewhere. This, too, will likely mean some additional cost, however, as the market maker seeks compensation for the risk transfer.

Some fixed-rate debt comes with prepayment penalties. You may be able to minimize their impact through up-front negotiation. However, once you're locked into the debt, you may incur additional cost to retire it early.

Cash Considerations

Interest-rate swaps settle much like swaps on commodities. An ISDA agreement usually governs how the settlement process works. Each swap is accompanied by its own paperwork establishing the values to be compared at settlement.

You may need to fund declines in value in advance of settlement through margin calls, depending upon your particular arrangement. Margin calls can be substantial and can therefore accelerate cash needs sooner than expected. Obviously, a cap contract with an up-front premium requires immediate cash. If you have tied your swap to the original debt by swapping with the lender, matching the index and term of the swap with those of the debt, the cash effect of the swap will be spread ratably across the remaining term of the debt.

Accounting Considerations

As with the accounting considerations for commodity hedgers, accounting can be the most difficult part of hedging interest cost as well. Generally, if you can trade your interest-rate swaps and caps with your lender and align the specifications of the swap with those of the debt, your accounting treatment will be simplest.

If you choose better economics over simpler accounting, you can expect some challenging discussions with stakeholders regarding the meaning of your financial statements. You can read more about this in Chapter 19. You'll do best if you get some expert advice to translate the meaning of the financial results for you. Your accounting firm may or may not be glad I sent you!

Financial Futures

As an alternative to interest-rate swaps, regulated exchanges offer financial futures to hedge against interest-rate changes.

Trading them will be simple—and will mitigate your counterparty risk. You'll also be able to exit them at will. However, designing an effective hedge that correlates well with your debt may be complex and challenging.

Financial futures contracts are premised on a static principal amount rather than a stream of payments on debt with declining principal. They are also forwarding-looking instruments whose value is subject to the market's perception of interest-rate changes over their entire term. Therefore, any interim change in value may not correlate well with the periodic change in the interest on your debt. Margin requirements may not correlate well with your cash flow, either. And accounting for them will be complex.

If you can align the remaining principal balance, remaining term, and rate index of your basket of debt with a financial futures contract, you can certainly reduce your business's interest-rate risk. You can also use these futures to manage short-term risk in advance of anticipated debt negotiations. Options on these futures offer yet another hedging tool.

When rates rise, the value of a financial futures contract will decline because it is premised on a fixed rate. Thus, you'll want to sell these contracts when entering into a hedge against rising interest rates, and buy them to close the hedge. When rates rise, the gain on the futures transaction will help offset your higher interest cost. Yet the complexity and difficulty of synchronizing these instruments with a business's debt makes them a challenging solution for less sophisticated businesses.

CHAPTER 11

Currency

*The world's supply of money speaks many languages. Be
wary of losing value in the translation.*

Here I am again, tossing another intangible commodity your
way. Virtually all businesses deal in some form of currency.
However, when you transact in two currencies, you'll need to
convert the foreign currency to the native one in order to
redeploy the funds in your business and report on your results.
The conversion exercise should remind you that currency risk
threatens your bottom line.

A Not-So-Foreign Concept

I remember vacationing in Canada many years ago. At the time,
the Canadian dollar was extremely weak compared to the US
dollar. Although the prices of goods and services there were
somewhat higher than comparable ones across the border in the
US, those vacations were economical. After I exchanged my US
dollars into Canadian dollars, I had more than enough money to
enjoy quality time in a foreign land!

Today, vacationing in Canada would be a bit more
expensive. The Canadian dollar has strengthened against the US
dollar. I wish I had saved some of those leftover Canadian
dollars, because I could now convert them into more US dollars
than I did many years ago.

Currency exchange rates change over time. Unlike inflation,
which gradually increases over time, the relative value of currencies fluctuates. Exchange rates ebb and flow. Only economists

can guess why they do. Some consider their relative values an indicator of the state of their respective economies. Regardless, **why exchange rates change is irrelevant from a hedging perspective. What's important is that they do change. And if you're holding assets or have commitments on the wrong end of a rate change, you're at risk for losing value.**

Any company that transacts business in more than one country's currency is at risk. If you pay to acquire or manufacture goods in currency A, and then you sell them in currency B, you may receive less compensation than you expect or need.

Currency Exchange Rate Futures

There's good news for those at risk. The futures market provides the necessary price discovery to educate you on the value of your goods and services in a foreign currency. Furthermore, you can trade those futures to lock in exchange rates, thereby protecting your business's value.

The foreign currency exchange futures, as you might suspect, quantify the relative value of two currencies. They price one currency's equivalency to one unit of the other currency. For example, a price quote on the CAD/USD contract shows the relative value of one Canadian dollar compared to one US dollar. A number less than one means the Canadian dollar is weaker than the US dollar. Any value greater than one means the Canadian dollar is stronger than the US dollar. For the current quotes for the CAD/USD contract, see http://www.cmegroup .com/trading/fx/g10/canadian-dollar_quotes_globex.html.

The math can be tricky until you understand how it works. It is more straightforward to convert from Canadian dollars to US dollars. Simply multiply the Canadian dollars by the exchange rate. To convert from US dollars to Canadian dollars, you need to divide the US dollars by the exchange rate.

If the CAD/USD exchange rate were 0.8000, you would receive $1.25 in Canadian money for every $1.00 of US money you exchanged ($1.00 divided by 0.8000). Since the Canadian dollar would be weaker, it would take more of them to buy something. If you had one Canadian dollar to exchange, you would receive 80 US cents in return.

Snowplows for Sale

Assume a US manufacturer contracts with a Canadian equipment dealer for sale of snowplows to Canadian municipalities. The contract anticipates delivering ten plows this time next year. Each plow will sell for $200,000 CAD (Canadian dollars), to be paid upon delivery. If today's exchange rate is 0.9000, each plow is worth $180,000 USD (US dollars). That's about what they sell for in the States, which makes sense because the US manufacturer wanted to convey the equivalent selling price to its Canadian customer.

Because the manufacturer produces its snowplows in US dollars, but will receive Canadian dollars in return, it has a currency exchange risk. There's a whole year before the manufacturer will be paid. Who knows what the exchange rate will be then? There's some uncertainty in this deal!

If the Canadian dollar weakens against the US dollar, the manufacturer will receive fewer US dollars. For example, if the exchange rate dips to 0.8000, the total contract value of $2.0 million in Canadian currency will bring only $1.6 million in US currency. That's $200,000 short of the $1.8 million sales value of the plows.

If, on the other hand, the Canadian dollar strengthens against the US dollar, the manufacturer will benefit because it will receive more US dollars. Nevertheless, management deems the risk intolerable. If they receive $1.8 million USD, they'll be happy. They'll have removed the uncertainty and placed this deal on par with their US business.

They decide to hedge the exchange rate, effectively locking it in at 0.9000 (the market's exchange rate for next year happens to be the same as today's exchange rate). To do so, they sell twenty futures contracts that expire one year from now. (The CAD/USD contract size is $100,000 Canadian dollars, as shown here: http://www.cmegroup.com/trading/fx/g10/canadian-dollar_contract_specifications.html.)

One year later, when the manufacturer delivers the plows, the exchange rate has dipped to 0.8500. At delivery, the manufacturer offsets its futures contracts by buying twenty of the same contract at 0.8500, a gain of 0.0500, or $5,000 a contract, $100,000 in total.

Illustration 11.1

Hedging Currency

	Dollars	Foreign Exchange Futures	Combined
Foreign sales dollars at risk	$2,000,000	-$2,000,000	$0
Exchange rate	0.90	0.90	
Expected domestic dollars	$1,800,000		
Exchange rate at delivery	0.85	0.85	
Domestic dollars collected	$1,700,000	$100,000	$1,800,000
Recap (in domestic dollars):			
Expected collections			$1,800,000
Collections without hedge			$1,700,000
Collections with hedge			$1,800,000

When the company collects from the dealer on the plows, the $2.0 million CAD selling price converts to $1.7 million USD using the 0.8500 exchange rate. That's $100,000 shy of what was needed based on the price for its plows in the US market. However, since the company hedged the exchange risk and gained $100,000 in the futures market, it ends up with the $1.8 million as originally anticipated, as shown in Illustration 11.1. The first column reflects the dollars collected from the deal before and after the currency exchange. The second column shows the gain on the futures contract.

Foreign Exchange on Consumables

If a US company purchases consumables in another country, using the foreign currency, it has the opposite currency price risk of that in Illustration 11.1. The dollars are flowing in the opposite direction. If the value of the foreign currency strengthens relative to the domestic currency, it will cost more US dollars to purchase the consumable. To hedge this exposure, the company would need a long position in the appropriate foreign currency exchange rate futures contract.

To illustrate, let's use the CAD/USD foreign exchange contract since we're already familiar with it. If a US company were buying $100,000 worth of potash in Canadian dollars from a Canadian producer, it would buy one futures contract. If the exchange rate went from 0.9000 to 0.8500 at delivery, the US company would lose $5,000 USD on the futures contract. However, with a more advantageous exchange rate of 0.8500, it would cost only $85,000 USD to purchase the raw material, even though the company anticipated spending $90,000 USD. The $5,000 hedging loss would bring the company back to its budgeted expenditure. There would be no advantage or disadvantage compared to the plan. The hedge would work perfectly by eliminating the risk of a change in the foreign exchange rate.

CHAPTER 12

Weather

When it comes to weather, either nothing is normal or everything is!

We now move into another dimension of hedging, but a significant enough one to warrant inclusion in a hedging book for businesses. This next risk isn't a price risk, and it may or may not be associated with the production or sale of a commodity. Yet the technique for hedging this risk is similar to that for hedging a commodity price risk. And, just like commodity price risk, this risk can bring dire financial consequences if left unattended.

Who's at Risk?

Weather risk is particularly challenging because it has multifaceted impacts. It can affect the demand for your products, the supply of commodities needed for your process, and certainly the price of commodities with any ties to your business. Those impacts can result in increases or decreases to supply, demand, and/or price. Most businesses have a capacity "sweet spot" where they run efficiently and profit optimally. Weather anomalies can cause under- or overutilization of their capacity. A thoughtful review of any business's weather risk will help in understanding whether to hedge it and how to hedge it.

What types of businesses might hedge weather risk?

A ski resort loses money when it doesn't snow. The resort may be able to make its own snow, but that costs money. Furthermore, there's marketing value to fresh snowfall, as the skiing public connects it with a trip to the ski slope. A weather derivative that pays the ski resort when snowfall is perilously low will help mitigate its risk.

A summer attraction, like a theme park or a golf course, stands to underutilize its earning capacity when it rains. Crowds dwindle. Beverage sales wane because of the cooler temperatures. A derivative that pays out when rainfall is above normal will help replace the missing contribution margin and cover some of the fixed costs.

Scorching-hot weather will imperil livestock. A rancher may seek derivatives that pay him when the temperature exceeds certain thresholds. Similarly, drought can have a catastrophic effect on crop yield. A farmer may want to trade his weather risk with that of a local theme park or golf course. Furthermore, the risk associated with the rancher's herd or the farmer's crop may be more than simply losing goods to sell. If either has hedged his price risk to lock in his profit margin (see Illustration 3.1), he is at risk for a futures loss if he has no physical commodity to deliver. The weather may make his commodity scarce, leading to higher prices and loss positions on short contracts. This bolsters the argument for an effective weather hedge.

When winter weather in the northeastern United States is warmer than normal, demand for heating oil weakens. Companies that market and deliver this oil will have difficulty covering their fixed costs or generating sufficient return on their investment. A weather-based derivative can lessen the warm-weather impact.

Weather Derivatives

Historical weather data create a baseline upon which hedgers and market makers can price and trade financial derivatives. Traders have a quantified normal against which to establish bid and offer prices. One's viewpoint on global climate change may create a debate about what is normal, but therein lies the art of negotiation.

Typically, weather derivatives are based on temperature and precipitation. You can trade either swaps or options. These financial instruments will trade specific to weather-measuring sites, most commonly airports, since clearly weather varies by location.

Two common variants of temperature are heating degree-days (HDDs) and cooling degree-days (CDDs). Energy providers use these indices as indicators for heating and cooling demand, respectively.

For example, HDDs are computed by taking an average of the daily high and low temperatures and comparing this average to a temperature threshold below which one would expect some demand for heating services inside of buildings (e.g., 60 degrees Fahrenheit). If last Saturday's temperature range was between 31 and 45 degrees, then last Saturday had 22 HDDs (average of 38 compared to 60). If the daily temperature range was between 58 and 65 degrees, there were no HDDs.

Essentially, HDD readings help quantify the degree of cold requiring heating services. Correlation between HDDs and demand for heating services is difficult to measure (as is the correlation between HDDs and profitability for heating service providers). Yet common sense and history suggest some degree of correlation, even though it is clearly imperfect.

The warm-weather equivalent to an HDD is a CDD. CDDs attempt to measure demand for air-conditioning. Since these indices have a documented history at many specific locations and indicate relative demand for heating and cooling services, they form the basis for hedging instruments for service providers.

An Example

When you trade any swap with a market maker, you agree to a swap level, which is a unit threshold that will help establish the value of the swap at settlement. When the units deviate from the swap level, one party to the swap will benefit at the expense of the other party. For swaps that hedge price risk, the swap level is a price. **For a weather derivative, the swap level may be denominated in inches, degrees, HDDs, or CDDs.**

For instance, you may agree to swap HDD readings at New York's LaGuardia Airport for the period from November to March, a typical "winter strip." As an energy provider who is looking for compensation when warmer than normal weather prevails, you might agree to a level of, say, 3,500 HDDs.

If the actual HDDs accumulate to only 3,000, you will receive money from the swap counterparty at settlement. This payout will help compensate you for a warmer than normal winter, when your business profits will be lagging. If the HDDs are instead 4,000, you will pay the counterparty. But that's okay because the colder weather will have helped your business make more money than expected.

Because the swap is not denominated in price, but rather by a numeric index, your swap agreement will define a value to establish the worth of one unit of measure (tick) in the swap. In our example, if the agreed-upon tick value is $400 per HDD, you will receive $200,000 at settlement ($400 x 500 ticks derived by comparing the actual 3,000 HDDs to the swap level of 3,500).

Assigning an appropriate tick value to a weather derivative is important because the tick value helps determine the payout. You want a tick value that approximates the effect on your bottom line when weather changes by one tick (e.g., one HDD). **If you can estimate how many product sales you will gain or lose for each tick, you can then convert your contribution margin per sales of product to dollars per tick.**

To illustrate, if your contribution margin is 40 cents per gallon of propane and you sell 1,000 fewer gallons for every one HDD shortfall, a tick value of $400 (1,000 x $.40) would restore the lost margin. You'll want to test all scenarios because you'll be paying out on colder weather. If you don't sell an additional 1,000 gallons for every HDD above the swap level, making 40 cents of·contribution margin for each such gallon, your hedge will be imperfect. You'll need to assess whether you can tolerate the imperfection under any scenario, given its likelihood.

Illustration 12.1 summarizes the preceding discussion.

It's unrealistic to expect perfection on a weather hedge—or on most other hedges for that matter. You're dealing with averages, and the correlation of earnings at different readings is going to be far from perfect. However, you'll certainly strive for a better result than when doing nothing, should weather go against you, provided the opportunity cost is reasonable for the risk you are hedging.

Illustration 12.1

Hedging Weather

	Weather Risk	Weather Swap	Combined
Assumptions:			
Projected quantity sales	4,000,000		
Projected fixed costs	$900,000		
Projected earnings (EBIT)	$700,000		$700,000
Contribution margin	$1,600,000		
Contribution margin per unit	$0.40		
Est. quantity loss per HDD	1,000		
Indicated tick value		$400	
Swap at normal HDDs		3,500	
Actuals:			
Actual HDDs		3,000	
Quantity and HDD shortfall	-500,000	500	
Lost contribution margin compared to swap gain	-$200,000	$200,000	$0
Total earnings	$500,000	$200,000	$700,000
Recap:			
Intended earnings			$700,000
Earnings without hedge			$500,000
Earnings with hedge			$700,000

Projections based on normal HDDs

Assumes actual earnings matched projections but for quantity shortfall

Best of Both Worlds

When hedging weather risk, you may prefer the concept of "weather insurance" rather than giving up the economic benefits when weather swings in your favor. With a swap, you willingly forgo some of those potentially handsome profits.

When considering how to hedge a capped-price sales program, how to limit exposure to increases in the cost of consumables, and how to cap interest cost, we've discussed best-of-both-worlds scenarios, when a hedger is willing to pay a premium to protect her risk without trading off the potential reward. An option will limit her exposure in the derivative to that up-front premium. It's no different with an option on a weather swap. When weather moves in your favor, you won't give away the business profits.

When hedging against warm weather, a heating services provider might willingly pay a premium to secure the right to swap at a predetermined strike price. Such an arrangement is akin to buying insurance. The insurance proceeds, however, are formula-driven and not subject to the conventional claims process.

In our example, the company would purchase a put option, which would allow it to swap the HDDs at an agreed-upon level (i.e., the strike price), should the actual HDDs fall short of that level. Since the premium is negotiable, the strike price of the option needn't be at an agreed-upon normal reading. Besides, **what one party considers normal the counterparty may not.**

In practice, a company may choose to self-insure the risk closest to the normal reading to help lower the premium. The less-likely-to-occur readings are further away from the normal reading anyway. In effect, the company will have just purchased catastrophic insurance.

Finding a Market

If you're looking for exchange-traded derivatives for weather, you'll find them only for major cities. If you're hedging weather risk at smaller locations, you'll need to seek over-the-counter markets. Since weather data are gathered and archived for most airports, traders can usually agree on the data and a swap price relative to that data.

Weather derivatives are not actively traded, even when listed on an exchange. There is little available price discovery. As discussed elsewhere, narrower markets tend to compromise the price a hedger will pay. The gap between the bid and the offer, or the proximity of each to the normal reading of the unit of measure in a swap, typically reflects this liquidity issue. Poor liquidity will invariably skew the swap level in favor of the party that is making the market for the hedger.

The market maker also has the upper hand in pricing an option on a weather swap. After all, the market maker is agreeing to assume the risk that you don't want. There may not be many other parties who want that risk, either, so be prepared to pay up to transfer it. Clearly, you have more to lose than the counterparty does by not trading the derivative, but you'll need to exercise some financial due diligence with respect to both pricing and counterparty risk. (See Chapter 16.)

To help assess the real cost of the hedge, you'll want to review the payout scenarios for several years of history. When you look at, for example, ten years of history, how much cash would have changed hands under the proposed derivative, and who would have received it? What would the average annual transfer have been? And, assuming there is a net cost to you, the hedger, is that cost necessary to stabilize business and keep lenders satisfied, or can you adequately self-insure the risk?

From my experience with price quotations on weather derivatives, favorable pricing is difficult to find. **If you can think of a business that has the opposite weather risk of your business, you may have found a trading partner who will have as much need to trade the instrument as you do,** leading to more equitable pricing. Share your data and your analysis with them to demonstrate both good faith and the benefit to both businesses. Be willing to swap at an equitable level to foster a long-term, mutually beneficial trading relationship.

Weather Derivatives, Complexities

While the theory of how weather derivatives help address weather risk is straightforward, complexities abound. Most of the complexities relate to how the instruments are valued and how they may correlate to a business's risks.

Perhaps the most common complexity with weather derivatives is to establish what is "normal." When you consider weather, either nothing is normal or everything is! However, normal to those who trade weather derivatives implies an average. Will you define normal as a ten-year average or as a thirty-year average? Will you throw out the high and low readings before computing the average? And how will your counterparty define normal? Once you've established normal, you'll begin the arduous exercise of trying to measure your business's contribution margin on either side of it.

Fine-tuning the correlation between weather and business results is difficult. Yet doing so will help determine the appropriate swap level and tick value (and premium for an option). It is easy to draw a conclusion such as "when it rains, my business loses money." However, **to execute an effective hedge, you'll need to understand the extent to which it loses money over an entire range of possible readings.** A simple weather swap assumes you lose (or make) the same amount of money for every single tick. Yet, realistically, a business's weather-related risk usually does not work that way. There are too many variables.

You may lose ten cents per pound when the actual rainfall is 90 to 100 percent of a proposed swap level, fifteen cents when it is 80 to 90 percent, and forty cents when it is 70 to 80 percent. Conversely, you may make fifteen cents per pound when the actual rainfall is 100 to 110 percent, and twenty cents when it is 110 to 120 percent, but you may lose ten cents per pound when it is 120 to 130 percent of the swap level. Calculating the correlation will be difficult enough. Knowing how reliable it is and just how to trade on it will be an additional challenge. Obviously, more than one weather derivative is indicated to hedge the above exposures, especially when rainfall exceeds 120 percent of the swap level.

Another issue with correlation between a business and a weather derivative is location. A derivative premised on one location in or near a business's markets may not reflect the actual weather readings at all locations in your business's footprint. For instance, a business hedging against inadequate snowfall in upstate New York with sites in Rochester, Lake Placid, and Binghamton may get unreliable results if it selects Rochester as a proxy for all three sites. The snowfall in Binghamton and Lake Placid may be far less than Rochester's, due to its lake-effect snow.

You may be able to build a composite of various sites to arrive at a representative reading for your entire footprint. A composite, however, may mask anomalies at any one of the multiple sites, leading to an inadequate payout on an option. If you want a composite, you'll need a market maker willing to trade it.

Variability in wind and sunlight will introduce additional imperfection in temperature-based weather hedges, particularly in cold weather. Wind and sunlight will influence energy consumption even though they may have little effect on HDD readings. Anybody with a poorly insulated home in northern Maine can tell you that wind chill affects the heating bill!

Some weather derivatives may uniquely define the unit of measure. For example, some swaps define HDDs by comparing the daily average of the high and low temperature to 60 degrees while others compare it to 65 degrees. You'll want to read the swap or option contract to confirm it meets your expectations before signing it.

One pitfall with weather swaps is the rounding convention used to compute the daily average. When you average high and low temperatures that total to an odd number, how is the 0.5 fraction handled? Is it rounded up, truncated, or not rounded? If it rounds up, actual degree-days will accumulate to a higher number, which will minimize the payout to a party who collects when HDDs are below the swap level. Statistically, the rounded-up HDD total will exceed the unrounded HDD total by 25 percent of the total days in the swap. If you have a favorable hedge with a 150-day swap term and a $400 tick value, rounding up will cost you $15,000! The devil, as they say, is in the details.

Some weather derivatives will settle monthly and some will settle as one strip of months. Depending upon the variability of the weather over the entire term, payouts on options could vary based on the settlement method. A payout is more likely with options that settle monthly, which should lead a market maker to charge a higher premium for them. Read the contract's fine print, consider the implications, and request changes where appropriate. Run the numbers before you sign on.

Is There "Snow" in That Crystal Ball?

When I first heard the terms *El Nino* and *La Nina,* and the weather theories connected with each, I thought an aggressive trader was trying to hoodwink me. However, scientific research suggests a correlation between these phenomena and precipitation and winter temperatures in various parts of the world. These weather patterns are indicated seasonally by analyzing temperatures of ocean currents off the coast of South America. I'll now reluctantly concede that *El Nino* and *La Nina* may provide some long-term visibility to anticipated weather patterns. They're even more likely to influence a trader's perception of a fair swap level.

You'll find that market makers may use weather trends or long-range forecasts to their advantage. Whether or not you subscribe to them, those prognostications can certainly influence pricing. I've reviewed many long-term weather forecasts, which I believe are speculative at best. As time goes on, however, better science may facilitate forecasts that are more reliable. Anyone who compares recent weathercaster results to those of yesteryear knows that meteorologists have improved their forecasting accuracy immensely. If that trend continues, weather derivatives will be priced out of existence!

*****

I hope the practical examples in this section have shed some light on how to address commodity price risk. In the pages that follow, we'll consider some secondary risks that arise when you hedge—and because you hedge.

SECTION IV

Hedging Risks

When you manage risks, you create more of them, albeit with less bite.

CHAPTER 13

Basis

Despite differences, working together beats the alternative.

What Is Basis?

Basis is one of the more challenging concepts when hedging risk. For purposes of our discussion, **basis represents any difference between the physical commodity at risk and the financial instrument used to hedge that risk.** Mathematically, the entire basis difference equals the price of the physical commodity minus the price of the hedging instrument. You'll hear the term "weak" or "strong" used to describe the absolute size of the negative or positive basis, respectively.

Basis is usually quantified by the difference between two price indices of the same or a similar commodity. If you purchase copper today for $3.35 per pound and hedge it with a futures contract at $3.37 per pound, your basis is -2 cents per pound. Basis comes in a variety of types, several of which may comprise the mathematical difference between the two indices.

While basis may not seem as material a component of price risk as the absolute change in the price of the commodity itself, it can nonetheless represent a significant cost—or opportunity. **You should evaluate basis risk with any hedge.**

Basis can arise due to differences in location, time, and product specification. There can even be differences in the indices used to compute cost, or in a business's contractual pricing for a given commodity. Sometimes these differences co-exist, sometimes not. Let's examine each of these types of basis separately.

Location Basis

Commodity futures contracts have a defined point of delivery. For example, one of the natural gas contracts delivers at the Henry Hub spur in Louisiana. If a business is hedging natural gas consumption in New York using the readily tradable Henry Hub futures, there will be a difference between the cost of the product in those locations. Why? Because (1) there is an implied transportation cost given the distance between the locations; and (2) there may be supply-and-demand differences in those two markets, which could translate into substantial price differences for the exact same product.

Buyers will pay a premium for a scarce commodity, and scarcity may simply be a function of location. While there might be plenty of product in one location, a transportation strike, a frozen harbor, or limited storage capacity may make product supply tight just a few hundred miles away. Since price is the great equalizer in the push-pull of supply-and-demand economics, **a commodity will price higher where it is scarcer, all other factors being equal.**

Time Basis

The price of a futures contract represents a forecast of a price at some time in the future. On June 15, the nearest futures contract for many commodities would be posted for July delivery because July is the closest future month. The price of gasoline is not likely going to be the same on July 1 as it is on June 15. Neither is it going to be the same in the month of November, when the peak demand of "driving season" has long since passed.

On US oil markets, potential hurricanes in the Gulf of Mexico will create large time basis differences between the various monthly futures contracts. The differences can become dramatic, and can cause unexpected hedging results even though the hedger may have selected the appropriate monthly contract when executing his hedge.

An immediate shortage of a commodity at a specific location can create both material time and location basis differences. The time basis exists because a near-term shortage can be rectified in a matter of weeks. Traders anticipate the easing supply ahead, and it is reflected in the lower futures price. **When a commodity's demand exceeds its supply, the nearer futures months will tend to trade higher than the more distant "back months" because the market anticipates that supply and demand will rebalance over time.**

Under normal market conditions, one might expect prices of a commodity in the future to be somewhat higher than its current price because there is an implicit time value of money and cost of storage factored into the futures curve. We learned about this back in Chapter 4, and applied it in Chapter 9. With an unlimited number of supply-and-demand factors amid an ever-changing business climate, it isn't difficult to see that a freewill marketplace will create unpredictable pricing differences in futures contracts.

Product Specification Basis

Sometimes the product specification of the futures contract that you will trade differs from the specification of the product whose price risk you are hedging. For example, the sulfur content of various grades of diesel fuel will vary depending upon the laws of the land where they are sold. Heating oil is essentially diesel fuel, but each may come with a different product specification, depending upon the jurisdiction. Because the products differ, so, too, will their prices. Yet these closely related products are often hedged using the same futures contract.

Hedging price risk using an index for a product with a different specification than the commodity you are hedging can be problematic, but you may have little choice. The futures exchange will list only so many products. Exchanges typically list products with more trading activity, to provide more efficient markets and fairer pricing to their clientele.

Heating oil is in high demand in the winter, when the weather is colder in the world's more populated and industrialized regions. Diesel fuel demand spikes in the summer, when consumption tied to travel tends to be higher. Although heating oil and diesel fuel derive from the same barrel of crude oil with only subtle qualitative differences, their supply-and-demand factors are unique. Hedging one with the other can present difficulties because the price of the physical commodity may or may not correlate well with the price of the futures or swap contract used in the hedge.

Likewise, interest-rate swaps come in a variety of shapes and sizes. Hedging the interest cost of prime-rate debt with a US Treasuries or LIBOR swap may not work well. Although all three indices measure interest cost, they are different products in unique debt markets. US Treasury and LIBOR rates also come in different strains, depending upon the duration of the associated debt, each of which will price uniquely.

Price correlation is an important factor to consider when selecting your hedging tool. **If the historical correlation of the two indices in your hedge suggests that much risk remains, you may need to supplement your hedge with a basis swap.** I'll explain basis swaps in more detail later in this chapter.

Index Basis

Sometimes, different indices attempt to quantify the price of the same physical commodity. They may just use a different methodology. Some may use end-of-day trades, some may use the average for the high and low trades of the day, while others may rely on quoted prices or hypothetical end-of-day settlement prices.

In the oil industry, vendors offering different pricing services will survey industry participants to quantify market prices on a daily basis. They may arrive at prices that vary for the same commodity delivered in the same market at the same time. A compilation of each vendor's daily price surveys forms an index upon which over-the-counter markets trade. Supplier contracts often use one of these indices to determine the cost of their customers' purchases. If a hedge is executed using a different index than what is used to purchase the commodity, an index basis difference will result.

Other differences arise when comparing actual contract cost to any of several indices. One's supply contract may not depend on any specific index, giving rise to yet another set of numbers for the same commodity. Just because your purchases do not rely on an index on which you can hedge does not mean that you cannot protect the price risk. Another index for the same or a similar commodity will likely provide an acceptable measure of price protection.

Why Is Basis Important?

Basis is an important facet in hedging because it introduces price correlation differences between the commodity and the instrument used to hedge it. Basis can cause unintended results, whether onerous or favorable. In extreme circumstances, those results can be worse than if you did not undertake a hedge in the first place.

Let's consider an example of how basis in hedging can impair an intended result. If you are hedging, with a futures contract, the cost of a commodity yet to be acquired for your manufacturing process, the cost of your actual commodity may have increased at a faster rate than the futures contract. If, when you purchased the commodity under your supply contract, its cost had increased by fifty cents, but the futures contract had increased by only forty cents, you'll be unable to recoup the ten-cent difference. You protected forty cents of the fifty-cent increase, so you're better off than if you did nothing, but you'll incur the unexpected ten-cent cost because the index upon which you purchased the commodity increased at a rate that exceeded the hedging instrument used to protect your risk.

Hedging Basis Risk

You can minimize basis risk if you are able to hedge your commodity price risk using the same index upon which you purchase the commodity.

In the above example, a supplier contract that allowed you to purchase your commodity based upon the futures index would have allowed you to purchase the commodity ten cents lower, thus mitigating the basis risk. However, because such a contract arrangement transfers some time basis risk to your supplier, in practice they may charge you a premium for this protection, which will cost you additional money when physical market prices are at or below those in the futures market. As an alternative to hedging with futures contracts, over-the-counter markets may offer you a favorable swap price on the same index used for purchases under your supply contract.

Sometimes, however, you may find no liquid hedging instrument priced using the same index that you used to purchase the commodity. Or, you may find such an instrument over the counter, but perhaps you prefer the execution, reporting, and credit-risk management advantages of a regulated exchange. So, you may want to use two hedging instruments to manage your risk.

When you use two hedging instruments in tandem to hedge one risk, you can realize the benefits of a regulated exchange for the majority of the risk, and then supplement your hedge position with an over-the-counter swap on the basis. Remember, basis is the difference between two indices rather than the absolute change in the price of one index. There is often higher risk associated with the index itself, because the basis may change little over the timeframe of the hedge. Odds are, you can trade a commodity efficiently and at fair prices using a futures contract on a regulated exchange. You can also manage and account for it more easily than an over-the-counter swap.

When you trade a basis swap and the swap value goes in your favor, the counterparty to your trade is agreeing to make up the difference between the change in two commodity indices from an agreed-upon starting point. If the basis swap value goes against you, you agree to pay the difference to the swap counterparty.

In the above example, let's assume that you and another party agreed to swap the basis at zero, meaning that you agreed the two price indices comprising the basis were to be equal for the duration of the swap. When the swap settles based upon the actual ten-cent difference during the swap period, you'll collect forty cents from the exchange when you cash up the futures contract, and ten cents from the entity that swapped the basis with you.

Illustration 13.1

Hedging Consumable and Basis

	Hedge with Paper	Physical Commodity	Combined
Quantity	100,000	100,000	
Price at start of hedge	$3.00	$2.99	
Price at delivery	$3.40	$3.50	
Increase in price	$0.40	$0.51	
Gain on futures contracts	$40,000		$40,000
Purchase physical at delivery		$3.50	
Expected purchase price		$3.00	
Loss on purchase of physical		-$0.50	-$50,000
Loss, net of hedge, without basis swap			-$10,000
Basis swap negotiated at start of hedge	$0.00		
Basis swap at delivery	$0.10		
Increase in basis swap	$0.10		
Gain on basis swap	$10,000		$10,000
Result, net of hedge, with basis swap			$0

Illustration 13.1 summarizes the use of a futures contract and a basis swap to hedge a consumable commodity price risk, using the assumptions described above. The futures contract and the basis swap needn't be entered into simultaneously, but they

should both settle at delivery of the physical commodity in order to provide a more "leak-proof" hedge.

In the above table, you may notice that the commodity price of $2.99 was lower than the $3.00 price of the futures at the inception of the hedge, the latter of which defines the expected purchase price of the commodity at delivery. The futures market was unwilling to match the current commodity price. The difference of a penny quantifies the basis between the physical commodity now and the market's perception of the price at a specific time in the future.

Also, notice that the basis swap was negotiated at even money ($0.00). The basis has its own forward-looking market. Although the basis today is a penny, the forward-looking market does not expect the same value at delivery, nor is it willing to trade at that price. The only way to recoup the penny is to buy the physical product today and hold it until delivery. However, it will likely cost more money to carry the inventory than the implied one-cent cost of the basis swap.

In practice, hedging basis may not be as simple as Illustration 13.1 suggests. As mentioned, the basis swap has its own forward-looking market, and the swap probably would not settle on the commodity purchase date. Furthermore, the entity that swaps the basis may not be willing to swap the basis at zero (meaning the parties would agree up front that the price of the futures and the price of the index used in the supply contract will be the same at settlement). And, as was explained in Chapter 8 under "Why Settlement Matters," any swap that settles on an average will render a different result than a contract that is traded at one point in time.

Sometimes you can work with the vendor from whom you purchase the commodity. Ask the vendor if it will alter its contract to allow you to purchase on the same basis as you hedge. You may find that you take on a premium for this service, but every risk has a cost. You've just had an indication from one party of the cost of the risk you are asking it to absorb for you. Then, you can decide whether eliminating the risk is worth the cost. Regardless, you now have a number to compare to that of another market maker, who may be willing to assume the basis risk at lower cost.

Exploiting Favorable Basis

You may encounter times when the basis of a commodity used in your business presents an opportunity to make money. When prices in forward markets allow you to lock in a favorable basis, you'll want to be prepared to execute. In Chapter 9, the discussion on the buy-hold-and-hedge strategy of inventory purchasing is a good example of exploiting favorable basis.

Foresight to opportunities like this usually exists because you already have, or can anticipate, business obligations with a basis risk. Eventually, you will execute hedges on those obligations or else self-insure the basis risk. **Exploiting the basis means that you will make your hedging decisions at what you judge to be the most opportune time, not just when the normal business cycle suggests you make them.** Basis value will be a major determinant of when you execute your trades.

Knowing how your hedging programs work and monitoring price levels in current and futures markets will allow you to recognize opportunities as they arise. Being able to execute on those opportunities in a timely fashion, however, may also require available cash, preauthorization from company management, and a willingness to deal with some administrative challenges, including record keeping, reporting, and hedge management. I've found that enhanced profits will usually cover a multitude of administrative challenges!

Another method of maximizing value on basis is to negotiate supplier contracts that will allow you to elect from any number of indices when purchasing a commodity. Obviously, the more purchasing options under such a contract, the better opportunity you will have to exploit pricing anomalies in those indices.

Otherwise, consider negotiating contracts with multiple suppliers to achieve similar flexibility. The first supplier may charge you based on index A; the second supplier may use index B. If you can purchase from the first supplier when the second supplier's price is higher, and vice versa, you'll achieve a lower overall purchase cost for the commodity.

You will likely be hedging price risk on all purchases of the same commodity using just one index, but that shouldn't stop you from minimizing your purchase cost. Good judgment can allow basis to work in your favor.

Concluding Remarks on Basis

Basis differences notwithstanding, the absolute price change in a commodity most often represents the largest component of commodity price risk. Just because basis introduces more complexity and price correlation issues that can undernourish your hedge—and your bottom line—don't conclude that the hedging exercise is a waste of time and money. It clearly is not, and has much to offer a prudent businessperson in stabilizing earnings and managing a significant business risk.

CHAPTER 14

Timing

Timing is everything!

What Is Timing Risk?

Commodity price risk exists because prices can change with the passage of time. Time, therefore, is a foundational component in hedging. **Knowing the period of time over which you will be at risk is crucial to making good hedging decisions because it will help determine which month's futures contracts you trade.** Getting the month right will reduce time basis risk.

Timing risk occurs when you've prognosticated the wrong delivery month and traded the wrong monthly contract. You now have a time basis difference that you didn't originally anticipate. As you approach delivery, or expiration of the contract you hold, it may or may not be correlating well with the commodity price in the correct month.

How to Deal with Timing Risk

The best method of addressing timing risk is to exercise diligence when preparing projections. Use accurate assumptions, build models thoughtfully, review calculations carefully, and apply the reasonableness test to them.

If possible, compare the data to prior period actual results. If your commodity is weather-sensitive, modify your historical quantities to take into account more normal weather patterns before comparing them to your anticipated hedging quantities for current periods. Consider, and adjust for, other events that may have thrown off the timing of delivery in the historical data.

The best time to address the timing risk is up front, when the price risk arises. If you trade a January futures contract when you should have traded a March contract, you can always roll the contract from one month to the other by selling one and buying the other, or vice versa, depending upon whether you are long or short. However, the price difference between the two monthly contracts may not be as favorable when you are closer to delivery as it was at the inception of the hedge. You may pay a penalty to keep yourself protected, particularly if there is a near-term imbalance in supply and demand. On the other hand, you may be lucky and realize an unanticipated benefit.

Conversely, if you trade a March contract when January was required, you may receive adequate protection from the March contract—or you may not. You'll want to retire the contract early if the quantities that gave rise to it were delivered early. Otherwise, after delivery occurs, you could be exposed to additional losses on a futures contract without earning an offsetting business benefit.

Timing risk can arise for business reasons, or from natural phenomena well beyond your control. **Weather, labor issues, counterparty contract defaults, or the economy in general can influence the delivery timeline.**

Hedging relies heavily on quantity estimates and average prices thereon. Your simulation of future events will take on new meaning when you trade contracts based upon your assumptions. When hedging, you will never arrive at the precise result you were anticipating. However, you should be in a better position, from a risk standpoint, than if you chose not to hedge at all. With respect to the commodity you are hedging, your net profits should approximate your expectations if you've estimated well.

CHAPTER 15

Volume

Estimation is an inexact science.

What Is Volume Risk?

Sometimes, not all of the quantity you anticipate when designing a hedge is delivered. If you've hedged more quantity than necessary, you will incur a gain or loss on some futures or options that will have no offsetting gain or loss in your business. That gain or loss will drop directly to your business's bottom line.

When you hedge a lower quantity than you actually deliver, you have only hedged a certain percentage of your price risk. You'll be exposed to any change in the commodity price on the quantity that was not hedged. Any adverse move in price will reduce your business's profit. A favorable move is a windfall.

How Does Volume Risk Arise?

Often, you will need to estimate the volume to hedge because no legal contract or business deal specifies the quantity at risk. You may be a farmer or a rancher trying to estimate yield. You may be a manufacturer trying to estimate consumption based on expected demand for your product. Or, you may be trying to predict how weather will influence your demand or supply.

When your quantity at risk is uncertain, you have a volume risk. That volume risk could crash your party on adverse price moves. You'll be exposed on the difference between the quantity you prognosticated (and hedged) and the quantity delivered.

Volume risk can arise even when you have a contract. If you offer your customers (or vendors) any leeway on quantities, you'll have volume risk. Once again, uncertainty breeds risk.

Naturally, if you botch the accounting and compute the incorrect quantity at risk, you may be unpleasantly surprised later when you discover that you hedged the wrong quantity. Double-checking your work, or having another person review it, may prevent needless errors from tainting your hedging program.

How to Deal with Volume Risk

With fixed-quantity contracts, you may be able to avoid volume risk. Make sure your contract penalizes the counterparty when a loss results because they have not honored their quantity commitment. Ideally, that penalty will approximate the gain or loss associated with the under- or oversubscribed quantity.

If volume risk is intolerable for your business, and you can't expect your customers to cover any hedging losses, you have another alternative to reduce risk. Utilizing options instead of futures for the quantity of your hedge that may never be delivered, or may be delivered in excess of your expectations, can reduce risk.

Long options, by their very nature, have limited risk. You'll pay an up-front premium to buy them, but nothing more. A futures contract, on the other hand, has unlimited risk. **If you are holding a futures contract that you later discover was unnecessary, you will lose money for every cent of adverse price movement on that futures contract.**

How might options address volume risk? When estimating the quantity at risk, consider a range of exposure. For example, if you estimate delivery of 1,000,000 pounds, and you have a high degree of confidence that you will deliver at least 850,000 pounds, but would never deliver more than 1,200,000 pounds, you can utilize futures for the minimum expected delivery of 850,000 pounds and then purchase options for the contingent exposure of 350,000 pounds. You will then have coverage under any expected scenario.

Options can be expensive, especially those with a long time horizon. You'll want to quantify the worst-case cost to assess whether the additional investment is prudent.

In many businesses, volume risk is simply part of being in the business. You'll want to minimize negative hedging results by taking proper precautions. Because of the inherent risk you and your competitors face, you may be able to price your products with sufficient profit margin to minimize the effect of negative volume variances.

CHAPTER 16

Counterparty

*When someone invites you to lunch, make sure he can
cover the bill!*

Who Is Your Counterparty?

When you enter into a hedge, some entity is on the other side of
your trades. That entity could be a client of another clearing firm
on a futures exchange, a financial concern (e.g., a bank,
investment firm, hedge fund, or insurance company), an
otherwise unrelated company within your industry, an existing
business partner, or even your client base.

**Knowing who has the obligation to perform financially
when you liquidate your positions is paramount. Of what
value is a hedge if you cannot ultimately collect on gains?
Furthermore, if you cannot trade, exercise, or price your
positions in a timely fashion, your results may be frustrat-
ing, disappointing, or worse.**

Credit and Performance Risks

Most counterparty risk pertains to the creditworthiness of the
entity on the other side of your trade. What counterparty is on
the hook is not always clear.

**Trading on a regulated exchange offers the most
comfort concerning counterparty credit risk.** As described in
Chapter 4, the exchange itself is backed by the combined
financial strength of its clearing members. When you trade on a
regulated exchange, the credit risk does not reside with whoever

took the other side of your trade, but rather with a financial giant intrinsically tied to the exchange itself. Given its design, essentially the exchange becomes the counterparty to all trades for credit purposes. This structure reduces the credit risk to a minimal and tolerable level for anyone who chooses to trade there. The exchange may not be offering you an ironclad guarantee, but it is pretty close.

Exchange rules spell out procedures and provide thresholds to determine daily accountability and transfer of cash. Because positions are monetized daily, participants are not allowed to accumulate debt in excess of their wherewithal. Since you have little to no risk that the exchange will not perform financially, you can focus on executing your hedge well. Therein lies your real risk.

An exchange's governance and history of executing trades reliably also gives you comfort that you will be able to trade in a timely fashion. And thanks to their daily reporting requirements, you'll always know the financial status of your positions.

There may be instances, however, when you are not able to participate on a regulated exchange. You may lack the volume or the financial capacity. Maybe it's simply impractical for you.

Instead, you may be tied to an existing business partner, such as a bank. Events in recent years demonstrate that not even banks are always a reliable credit risk. If you already owe your business partner more than you anticipate that entity owing you on a hedge, then your credit risk with that entity may be moot. However, if that entity goes bankrupt, you may or may not be able to offset any opposing debts. A lawyer can help you understand your risk on specific deals.

If margin, or collateral, is required to support your over-the-counter positions, make sure the flow of cash is bilateral. If you are required to send money when your positions go against you, is there some way to recoup those dollars should prices reverse before settlement? Conversely, if the position goes in your favor, why shouldn't your counterparty send you cash before settlement? After all, it is a "swap."

Some market makers may take a hard stand on the bilateral flow of cash. If a partner is not legally obligated to send you cash, and is unwilling to do so, you might wonder what that partner is doing with your money before settlement. Check around for the best deal. Although a below-average credit standing may deny you this privilege, access to cash should be one of your criteria in selecting a trading partner.

Sometimes you may trade some standardized instruments over the counter even though they are listed on a regulated exchange. In those cases, you may be able to transfer these instruments to the exchange, effectively transferring your counterparty credit risk from the OTC trading partner to the exchange.

Recent law changes in the United States have created a class of OTC trading whose credit backing works like that for exchange trading. Essentially, credit risk management for this class is subject to more regulation, and your credit risk spreads to a larger group of market participants, providing you with a higher level of comfort.

Due Diligence

What if you are trading with an unfamiliar entity? **One of the more significant considerations with over-the-counter trading is to know the financial condition of the party with whom you are trading, as well as that party's reputation, timeliness, and reliability.** You'll want to understand your trading partner's ability to perform on your behalf. The inability to collect on hedging gains may bring you to the untimely realization that you really had no hedge at all.

You have the right to perform your own credit assessment and reference check on any trading counterparty, and you should do so. These are reasonable due diligence measures. Any firm that does not cooperate should be disqualified. Online searches can provide an added level of comfort, especially with public entities, which are required to disclose more information.

Make sure you note the legal name of your counterparty, the one that appears on paperwork such as an ISDA agreement or a proposed swap contract. This is the entity whose creditworthiness you should examine. Sometimes large corporations establish separate legal entities to run their trading groups, even though they are referred to casually as the more recognizable name of their parent or sister corporation. If those entities look to the larger corporation to pay their bills, you may want to seek a financial guarantee from the deeper-pocketed organization. Otherwise, the trading partner needs to demonstrate that it is financially strong enough to honor its financial commitment, should any trade go in your favor.

When you call a reference to check a trading partner, ask the reference specific questions. Prepare these questions in advance of your call. You might consider the following: *Have you ever had a dispute and, if so, how was it resolved and was it resolved to your satisfaction? How often does this trading partner provide you with quotes that are not competitive with other market makers? How often is this trading partner unavailable to service a request, and how long does it take this trading partner to call you back? What is your biggest complaint with this trading partner?*

Taking the time up front to assess your trading partner may save you some headaches down the road. There are more alternatives available to you than may seem apparent at the outset. Ask around and find a few trading partners who are right for you. Be wary about putting all your eggs in the same basket when it comes to over-the-counter trading.

CHAPTER 17

Cash

All earnings ever recorded hinge on this one commodity.
Make sure you have enough of it when you need it most.

Cash risk? I thought that might get your attention! Risk of insufficient cash flow might be a more precise phrase. Regardless, the timing of the cash payments on financial instruments used in hedging is a significant factor to consider before entering into trades. Here's why.

Trading on Margin

As I touched on in Chapter 4, when you trade futures contracts on a regulated exchange, you need an underwriter, an entity that understands your financial capacity and stands behind your trades. You work with a broker, who, along with the clearing member firm, assesses your creditworthiness, places appropriate and relevant limits on your trading, and manages cash flow for your account. Your clearing member firm will hold futures (and options) positions and cash collateral on your behalf. It also provides the necessary funding to the exchange for all losses incurred on those positions.

You will trade futures on margin, which means you fund only the portion of the contracts deemed at risk for financial loss in the near term. The broker communicates that information to you daily, based on the underwriting of your business.

When you begin trading, you fund your position by transferring some collateral, often cash, to your account with the clearing member. The clearing member, in turn, manages the cash flow to support your positions with the exchange.

Several factors influence your margin requirements. In addition to your own creditworthiness, the clearing member assesses the risk of your positions by considering the risk of the underlying commodities. The size of your position and the potential daily price changes of the particular commodities are considered. Each commodity contract has an estimated daily exposure, established by the exchange, which helps determine the clearing firm's daily exposure and therefore the collateral requirements. Since the clearing firm actually holds the contracts on behalf of its client, it is ultimately liable to the exchange. You, the end client, are liable to the clearing firm.

When the price of your positions moves against you, you sustain losses that reduce your margin account. When your margin account dips below a minimum threshold, the clearing firm will issue a "margin call." A margin call is a request for you to replenish your collateral immediately, usually to a "maintenance" level well above the minimum threshold. A margin call may even take into consideration a change in the required collateral due to a change in market conditions or the approach of expiring contracts.

Typically, margin requirements on accounts are assessed daily. Because cash transfers on loss positions are also expected daily, money is wired or otherwise transferred by some mode of electronic funds transfer (EFT) to ensure timely receipt. If your futures positions move in your favor, resulting in gains, you may be entitled to receive those monies in excess of your positions' collateral requirement, depending upon your particular arrangement.

If you do not pay a margin call timely, you run the risk of the clearing firm closing your positions and keeping the portion of your collateral required to cover the losses. Not only will you have incurred those losses, you will forfeit the ability to recoup them, should market prices reverse. Furthermore, you may lose additional money on the physical commodity, since you no longer have a hedge in place.

Closing a hedge in midstream, whether by choice or by default, can be worse than if you had not hedged in the first

place. You can lose money on the hedge instrument, and then you can lose more money on the commodity.

The more futures positions you hold, the more collateral will typically be required. If you hold opposing positions (i.e., long and short positions in the same commodity, perhaps in different delivery months), those positions will likely offset one another when determining collateral requirements, although higher margin requirements may apply on soon-to-expire contracts.

For example, you may own five long May corn contracts and seven short July corn contracts. Your margin requirements will be computed based upon holding two "net contracts" rather than twelve total contracts. Potential losses on five of the seven July contracts will be offset by gains on the May contracts, and vice versa.

Potential Cash Crunches

Due to the nature of trading on margin, there can be instances when the demand on your cash places a strain on your short-term supply of it. You may need to work with a banking partner or pledge noncash assets as collateral. Or, you may need to consider alternatives to hedging through a regulated exchange, such as an over-the-counter trading arrangement in which your trading partner can help bridge cash needs. You'll want to anticipate any possible mismatches between the cash flow from the hedging activity and the cash flow from the transactions you are hedging.

For example, you may be hedging a fixed-price sale of a commodity before your customer pays you. In order to lock in your expected profit margin, you purchase a long futures position to offset the sale to your customer. You'll immediately need to post collateral for that position. If the price declines before you deliver the product and before your customer pays you, you'll need to send more collateral to cover the losses on the futures contracts.

To fund your margin account, is it possible to place a clause in the customer's contract requiring an up-front deposit or accelerating a portion of the sales proceeds in the event the commodity price falls? You'll certainly make up those losses— and then some—when you collect on your customer's account (assuming you can). After all, your selling price won't decline. However, absent any provision for cash advances from the customer, you may experience a cash crunch before you deliver the goods.

By the very nature of a hedge, a negative position in your futures contracts suggests a positive position in your physical commodity. If you are not able to monetize the favorable physical position at the same time that you must fund losses on the futures contracts, you may have a short-term cash crunch. That's when a financial partner can help bridge the cash shortfall.

You may be operating in a jurisdiction that requires you to escrow customer deposits. If so, you'll have even less cash to fund your margin account. Any additional margin calls resulting from adverse price moves before you deliver and collect your customer's cash will stretch your cash, or send you to the bank for a short-term loan.

Cash Flow for Options

Because option values deteriorate over time, you will typically be required to fund the entire premium associated with long options up front, when you purchase them. This causes an immediate demand on cash that you may not have collected yet from the business deal that necessitated the options.

You also may or may not be entitled to recoup any of the intrinsic value of an option before it is exercised, depending upon the rules of the exchange and your arrangement with your broker. Choosing to exercise a deep-in-the-money option before it expires may release some incoming cash, but you will have lost the one-way price benefit of an option before its time. A subsequent price reversal will trigger a margin call on the futures contract that resulted when you exercised the option. You will end up unexpectedly losing money if the reversal in the futures price eclipses the option's intrinsic value when you exercised it. Had you known that, you would never have exercised the option in the first place.

OTC Cash Implications

Some over-the-counter hedging trades on margin, some does not. The same cash crunch considerations described above could pertain—or be avoided. Read the legal paperwork carefully for the cash implications. Better yet, **strategize up front and request cash-friendly contract modifications before signing.**

Your banking partners and your suppliers may be good trading partners if they can price your commodity competitively with the broader market. They both have a stake in your success (and you in theirs). Furthermore, you already know the players and should have a good working relationship with them. They already know your business. You may be able to take advantage of existing credit lines to cover any cash exposures pertaining to your hedges.

As alluded to in Chapter 5, some regulated exchanges may accept transfer of positions in certain commodity contracts traded over the counter. Those contracts must be standard and listed as transfer-eligible by the exchange.

Transferring OTC trades to the exchange allows you to seek better pricing from a wide variety of market makers. You're no longer constrained by their creditworthiness because you'll be relying on the relatively low credit risk of the exchange. Your relationship with these market makers may begin and end with the trade at hand.

Another advantage of transferring OTC positions to an exchange is to consolidate your positions for both reporting and margining purposes. This leverages the relationship you already have with the exchange. Your administrative staff will thank you for simplifying their cash management and record-keeping duties.

Closing Thoughts on Cash Risk

Just as you should always be mindful of who will be paying you, and their ability to do so, you need the same mindset when you incur a loss on a hedging instrument. As a hedger, you'll be collecting some offsetting benefit from your business. Who will fund that benefit? Are they contractually bound and do they have the wherewithal to perform? It's a real risk, and it is more than just a short-term timing issue.

Collection risk is not new to businesses. However, it can be worse under certain hedging scenarios. When the commodity price goes against you, it may also have gone against your customer. Hindsight is always 20-20, and your customer now knows he could have gotten a better deal—or still could elsewhere. He might be tempted to renege on your deal and buy his commodity from your competitor at a lower market price, leaving you stuck with your hedging loss. Not only do you lose the ability to recoup your hedging loss, you also lose the profit you expected to earn from his business. **Make sure you are diligent about binding customers to their deals.** Put some sharp teeth in your contracts and consider mandatory cash deposits.

In some cases, you may even want to require a standby letter of credit to protect your business interests. A standby letter of credit will allow you to collect from your customer's financing partner when an agreed-upon event takes place.

As with many facets of hedging, forethought is important. **If you don't have the cash needed to float your hedge program, you'll need to design another one.** Just as you check the weather forecast before setting sail on open waters, you can't afford to be in the midst of a hedge and be forced to "pull the plug." You won't be happy with the results—unless you're just plain lucky. And you might just sink the boat.

CHAPTER 18

Execution

Even the best of plans fail if you don't pay attention to the details.

The first step in any hedge program is to understand your business's risks. **Until you can effectively define the problem, you won't find an effective solution, and you'll have trouble measuring how your hedge performs.** Once you've developed a good comprehension of your risks, you'll be in a better position to design, implement, and track sound hedging strategies.

Maybe you already have outstanding strategies, but the results aren't as expected. When it comes to executing your program, is there a breakdown? You can increase your chances for success if you have the right people and the right organizational structure.

Personnel Matters

It really does matter. You need people with the right skills performing the critical tasks. In hedging, the stakes can be high, and the skills can be difficult to find. If you're a particularly small business, executing a hedge can really be challenging because the hedging function may need to be just one part of someone's job. Here are some qualities to look for in that person.

Does the candidate understand your business well enough to know the risks? That's vital. If you don't understand risk, you won't understand how to manage it.

Is your candidate trustworthy? I know, you trust all of your employees, or they wouldn't be your employees. But trust in a hedger must go to another level. Not only is this someone who wouldn't steal from you or lie to you, this is someone who is true to his word and who won't be swayed emotionally when market conditions toss some tempting "bait" his way. Some people have a propensity to gamble, while others have an overwhelming need to be liked, if not celebrated. In a weak moment, your candidate may end up as goat instead of hero, dragging you down with him!

Does your candidate take ownership of his job? Or is he just collecting a paycheck? As a hedger, he will be living his job because commodities trade around the clock. **Do you have confidence that your candidate won't let you down?**

You're looking for someone who is both steady and sharp. A hedger needs strong analytical skills. He'll be dealing with complexity and math on a regular basis. And he will need to be quick on his feet and not crack under pressure. If he doesn't have these qualities today, does he have the potential to develop them quickly, once he's been in the hot seat for several weeks? If not, you have the wrong person.

Even if your hedging needs are limited, you'll still want some backup. Who will execute trades when the hedger is not available? And, what if you lose her? Eventually you will. Hedging requires daily attention. Quantities at risk change constantly. Expiring contracts that are not offset place you in the awkward position of needing to fulfill a delivery obligation that you may be unprepared to do. Chances are, you can't afford to let that happen. It's best to groom a successor while you have someone with experience to train him.

Because of the analytics and financial implications involved, you might already be utilizing someone in your finance department to hedge your risk. If your organization is large enough, involving another employee with accounting expertise will be helpful, too. This individual will unravel the activity from brokerage statements and record transactions. Having an employee who understands the hedge program well and who knows how to structure the accounting will go a long way in helping you understand hedge performance. It will also strengthen your company's internal controls, its backup, and its knowledge.

Outside Assistance

It is always beneficial to seek outside assistance on your hedge program. If you isolate yourself, you can become stale. You need fresh ideas and current information. Hedging is part art and part science. There may be more solutions than meet the eye. Having input from others in the industry can help stimulate creativity and uncover opportunities.

One great source of input is daily contact with a quality broker. A good broker will understand the market pulse and keep you apprised of market-moving news. Canned research reports and emails aren't enough. You need someone who knows your programs and can reach out to you when unusual events are driving the market.

Your broker should have connections. She can offer advice on hedging strategies or connect you with various over-the-counter market makers for custom hedges. Brokers can offer a wealth of knowledge and resources. They come with different strengths and personalities. If you can tap into their experience, you'll learn much.

You'll want a broker you work well with. Don't be overly concerned with commission rates as long as they are reasonably competitive. **A broker's commissions are relatively small compared to the value she can bring you and the hedging gains or losses you may incur.** Also, be sensitive to how your broker may resolve disputes. You will have disagreements from time to time, and you'll want someone who does the fair and right thing. It's a good indicator of whether she'll advocate for you even when you're not looking over her shoulder.

Periodically, you may also benefit by sharing your hedging challenges with industry peers. Keeping in contact with market makers will help keep you abreast of developments and may provide you with more competitive pricing on deals down the road. You'll also glean useful information from others with more experience and knowledge.

If you're really stuck, or you just want an expert opinion on how you're doing, engage an independent consultant to look at your risks and your hedging programs. Look at the fee you will pay him in the context of the dollars you have at risk. Good advice will pay for itself many times over.

Oversight and Controls

When is the last time you reviewed your hedging results? Have you developed reports that offer a quick read on hedge performance? Or are you trying to extract those results from your monthly profit-and-loss statement, or worse yet, your brokerage statement? It is important to have reports that will monitor the performance of each hedge program. Those reports should synchronize with your accounting books to ensure their accuracy.

How does your hedger monitor the quantities at risk? She needs that information daily to adjust the hedge. If your futures and physical quantities don't match, you're still at risk. If you can automate your accounting systems to identify your quantity at risk, and archive the report daily, you'll have the information you may need later to find out why a particular hedge did not perform well, or why one did. In-house information technology expertise is a distinct advantage in maintaining an effective hedging function. It can also help in complying with recent regulations imposed upon hedgers. If you cannot produce automated reports, then computer spreadsheets will need to suffice.

Without information that properly identifies your company's risk, you will have difficulty managing your hedge optimally and assessing the results. **Remember one of the most important premises for hedging: know your risk!** Once you have some data that identifies it, make sure you read it. And make sure you back it up!

Do you have procedures in place to authorize broad hedge strategies? Who is involved in those decisions? You'll want to assemble a brain trust with sufficient diversity and authority to make balanced, yet timely and informed decisions. Don't involve too many people in this process, because time is a critical facet in hedging. I would suggest no more than four voting members, with three yes votes required to authorize decisions. Concise email documentation will be an important reference tool to remind people months later of the decisions that were made and why.

Do your employees know what you expect of them? Have you clearly communicated your strategies? Are there adequate controls on how the hedge function is to run? You don't want to tie your hedgers' hands because they may need to be nimble as opportunities present themselves. Yet they also need to know their limitations. For example, do certain types of trades require the approval of additional people in the organization? And if action is taken without the proper approvals, what are the repercussions?

Your broker can (and will) help you establish controls on trading. When you set up an account, she'll ask what types of trading you will do, including the commodities and quantity exposures. If you try to enter a trade for a commodity you aren't authorized to trade, or in a quantity that exceeds acceptable limits, the trade should be rejected.

Trades should be logged immediately when they're executed. Every day, you should verify prior-day trades against your brokerage statement for contract, price, and quantity. If your broker offers the service, you may be able to perform this verification for current-day trades by the end of the day.

Inform your broker of any discrepancies immediately so they can be resolved in a mutually agreeable fashion. Regardless of the medium, communication is not perfect. Neither are people. You'll want to advocate your position while exercising sufficient grace to ensure your broker is still eager to serve you.

Are you placing online trades? If so, who has access to the login credentials? And how are they safeguarded?

Have you segregated the duties of the hedger from those who manage the cash and from those who report on the results? If you're quite small, this may not be practical. In that case, you might want an outside accounting firm to periodically review controls and performance, if not audit the results.

Because of the inherent risk in the hedging tools themselves, key stakeholders, such as lenders and investors, will want every possible assurance that the tools are managed well in the context of your business's risks. They will gain comfort when you formalize your controls into a hedging policy. After all, one misinformed or disgruntled employee can inflict significant financial damage when given unfettered access to your hedging account. **Documenting your controls will help demonstrate that your hedging program has been designed thoughtfully and is executed with discipline.** The policy itself is an additional control, as it becomes the playbook for the hedging function even as personnel change. Even the very development of the policy can force you to consider what controls may be lacking in your program.

Developing a hedging policy can become quite involved, and is beyond the scope of this book. The policy should be tailored to your particular business. If your operation is large enough to warrant a more elaborate policy, obtain a boilerplate policy from a third party within your industry to see what is included. Your broker, an industry group, and other hedging partners may also be sources of some working samples.

Giving thought to and implementing proper controls will help ensure that what you think is happening is really happening. Don't let great strategy be undone by poor implementation. Although details can be cumbersome and may seem extraneous, you won't want to find out the hard way that they are indeed necessary.

SECTION V

Hedging Wrap-up

A hedger whose scorecard reads as expected has done well. It's not about making money. It's about managing risk.

CHAPTER 19

Accounting for Hedges

*If you don't keep score, you'll never know how you're
doing. (Even when you do keep score, you may still
struggle to know what it all means!)*

Congratulations! You dared venture into this chapter. Some
might call you a glutton for punishment, but I commend you for
your persistence and for your willingness to learn. Whether
you've digested well what I've already thrown your way or
choked on it, you can at least thank me for saving the nastier,
bone-filled morsels until last.

What you'd really like to see on a set of financial statements
are numbers that demonstrate you have achieved your hedging
goals. Expectations will vary based on your particular facts and
circumstances, but if we accept the premise that hedging is
designed to eliminate the financial impact of fluctuations in
commodity prices, then **one would expect earnings over time
that resemble a bicycle tour through the plains of North
Dakota rather than a roller-coaster ride on the Cyclone.**

Preamble

You're about to enter a discussion on a complex, highly
technical topic. To do justice to accounting for hedges would
require a much deeper dive than I've taken here, which is
beyond the scope of this book. However, some coverage of the
topic is appropriate to acknowledge the official bookkeeping for
hedging and to alert readers to some of the associated hazards.

In short, here's what this chapter communicates. Would-be hedgers should realize they face a choice in how to account for their hedges. With their accounting firms by their side, they should carefully evaluate whether attempting to comply with hedge accounting pronouncements is worth their time and expense or whether simply avoiding the technical requirements and accepting the consequences is more beneficial. Those consequences will likely require additional measures to satisfy all of their stakeholders.

With this chapter summary now in hand, and before I venture any further, I'd like to offer additional context for the following discussion. There are perhaps two types of businesses out there with hedging needs.

First, there are those whose hedging exposures are important enough to warrant some thoughtful hedging strategies, yet whose hedging gains and losses do not rise to a material level compared to the profit and loss of their entire business. Hedging may be peripheral to what they do, or perhaps they are hedging in commodities with less price volatility than others have. For this group of businesses, I say, "Read on—and be thankful that you're not part of the second group."

For the rest of you, I don't mean to sound alarmist, but you have some reporting challenges on your hands. You might be engaged in a business for which commodity price risk is central. In fact, you may sell exclusively one commodity. Or, perhaps you deal with a commodity prone to wild price swings (and there are several of those). Your hedging activity is very material to your overall financial performance. To you, I say, "Grab your fork and steak knife and read on!"

The Hard Part

I once spoke with a consultant who ran his own commodities trading firm. He was engaged to advise us on the company's hedge program. When I asked a question about the accounting, he paused, sighed, and then said, "I don't know about the accounting. That's the hard part."

In my experience as a hedge strategist, one who placed orders, and someone charged with explaining the results, I can't agree more with the latter part of the consultant's comment. The accounting is the hard part . . . for a couple of reasons.

Traditional accounting systems like to compute cost of sales based on actual invoices and related cash disbursements. They don't typically take hedging gains and losses into account. Indeed, identifying the true cost of a hedged sale can be challenging enough.

To complicate matters, the accounting establishment, the folks who run the US-based Financial Accounting Standards Board (FASB), also don't make it easy to include hedging gains and losses in cost of sales, at least not in a fashion that matches the gain or loss with the earnings of the hedged commodity itself. Accounting rules have traditionally done a commendable job of matching revenues and expenses, but not here. They impose onerous requirements for hedgers to achieve the logical accounting treatment. Consequently, readers of financial statements may find it challenging to assess the profitability of a company and to know whether it has made or lost money on specific hedge programs.

The reporting company's difficulty arises in determining what constitutes hedging. The FASB requires extensive tracking and testing of the hedge instruments compared to the items they purportedly hedge. This exercise determines whether you are hedging, and the extent to which you are hedging. I know that wasn't in doubt in your mind. However, in this court of law, you are guilty until you prove yourself innocent. To do so could be both time-consuming and expensive. Yet without complying, profit margins—and earnings—can be grossly misleading in short-term reporting periods.

Many small businesses cannot afford to invest in the resources and staffing needed to comply with the accounting regulations for hedging. They're busy trying to make money rather than spending the time to fine-tune the reporting of it.

Noncompliance with FASB's hedge accounting regulations forces the would-be hedger to mark all futures and options positions to end-of-period market settlement prices, and to ram the gains and losses through the current period's income statement. Yet gains and losses associated with the commodity itself are not recognized until the events that would earn such income or incur such cost have occurred, as traditional accounting rules require. Delivery is one such event.

What can result is a balance sheet and an income statement with surprising numbers. In some price scenarios, a company might report a net loss—or an overblown gain—on their entire operation's bottom line when none has really occurred. Why? Because **the financial effect of a large price change of a commodity-based derivative, when segregated from the change in the value of the physical commodity that derivative is designed to eliminate, can dwarf the company's net income.** An unsuspecting reader might draw the wrong conclusion—especially without combing the financial statement footnotes for disclosures of mismatched gains and losses.

Eventually, when the hedged commodity is delivered and its earnings or cost is recognized, any previously recognized hedging gains or losses will have missed their long-lost cousins. They lived at another time, on an earlier set of financial statements. Meanwhile, the bottom line on the latest income statement will also raise eyebrows. (See Illustration 19.1 near the end of this chapter.)

Because stakeholders often do not understand the complex nature of hedging instruments—and thanks to the negative publicity surrounding abuses and the perception that futures and options contain an element akin to high-stakes gambling—there is often a suspicion of sins buried within hedging results. And if there were indeed any to be hidden, there could certainly be plenty of cover there.

Even for companies with a history of integrity and transparency in reporting, the perception described above will probably not change. Embarrassed by high-profile reporting scandals in past decades, and with the public watching as the US Congress applied a higher level of scrutiny, the self-policing accounting industry went overboard with stringent regulations. Essentially, every embedded gain or loss on a financial derivative must be recorded through the financial statements. The new rules may have been developed with the right motivation and good theory, but they are difficult to comply with on a practical level, especially for small businesses.

The net result? Gains or losses are often recorded in the wrong period—that is to say, they are recorded in a different period than the counterbalancing activity is. Ironically, the Internal Revenue Service's treatment of hedge accounting—that used for US income tax reporting—is less tedious than the accounting industry's.

What Is Hedge Accounting?

Hedge accounting is an accounting treatment afforded to those who spend the time and expense to demonstrate that their hedging instruments qualify as such. It will allow hedgers to defer the recognition of gains and losses on futures and options until the delivery of the hedged items (when their associated income or cost is recognized). This matching will better reflect hedge performance. Financial statement footnotes will disclose any remaining gains and losses on derivatives not yet recognized through the company's income statement.

Separate rules are imposed on US businesses versus non-US businesses. The FASB has jurisdiction over US businesses, and I will focus my discussion there. What are some of the onerous requirements I've been referring to? Let me briefly address three relevant issues stemming from the FASB's hedge accounting rules:

- Designation of hedge items
- Measurement of hedge effectiveness
- Price correlation

I'll provide some commentary about each, but a more thorough discussion of these regulations, as well as rules for non-US businesses, is beyond the scope of this book. The International Accounting Standards Board (IASB) sets standards for non-US reporting. Regulations have a way of changing over time. You should check postpublication developments in the accounting rules to assess their impact.

When a business enters into a hedge, the accounting regulations would have it assign the specific hedge instruments to the specific units of the commodity whose price risk they are designed to hedge and then track hedge performance to delivery. For example, when an oil refiner purchases a cargo of crude oil and enters into a hedge by selling crude oil futures contracts, the regulations require it to tie those particular futures contracts to those particular barrels of crude oil. Yet, under other accounting regulations, traditional inventory cost flow assumptions, such as first-in-first-out (FIFO), last-in-first-out (LIFO), or average cost, do not utilize this specific identification approach.

Tracking a hedge by specific identification may not be feasible in certain industries, particularly when the commodity is comingled with prior purchases and lacks specific identity apart from those purchases, such as oil stored in a tank or grain in a bin. When some of the sales from that stockpile have other hedging exposures, such as fixed-price or capped-price sales, the task of specific identification becomes even more unwieldy.

Even the estimated timing of sales can cause difficulty in building a traceable hedge. For instance, when customer demand is highly dependent upon swings in the weather, choosing when the specific lots of a commodity will be delivered can be virtually impossible. One might rather make judgment calls, based on the shape of the futures curve, about which futures months to sell to protect an inventory's value, and reposition the hedges further into the future as contracts approach expiration. From a practical standpoint, the daily exercise of some hedgers is not to figure out which units were bought and sold, as the hedge accounting regulations prescribe, but rather to determine the total quantity of inventory at risk, to ascertain whether it increased or decreased from the prior day, and to adjust the overall size of the hedge accordingly.

The accounting regulations also mandate a detailed measurement of what they refer to as hedge effectiveness. From my experience in dealing with heating oil, the tolerance for deeming a hedge effective seems quite rigid. Effectiveness, mind you, has nothing to do with whether hedges are generating adequate compensation to cover the price risk. Rather, the term pertains to mathematical correlation of price. The two components of hedging results, effective and ineffective, must be quantified, likely requiring actuarial expertise. Most small businesses will not go to that extent. There are other more critical needs competing for their limited budgets.

A review of price correlation trends between many commodities and their associated hedge instruments might clarify the feasibility of achieving hedge accounting treatment. Basis issues alone can push correlation well below the required threshold. You, like others, may find that chasing an accounting treatment whose benefits you may be unable to realize is not worth your time or money.

Ultimately, you must prove that you can comply with FASB's criteria for hedge accounting if you wish to use this method of accounting, and you will likely want to do this only with your accounting firm's stamp of approval. If the stringency of the hedge accounting criteria leaves you dead in the water, you will want to find an effective method to communicate financial results to your board, your shareholders, and your bankers, a method that elucidates the economics of your hedging activities.

No Hedge Accounting? Now What?

Meanwhile, you'll likely still want and need your financial reporting to comply with Generally Accepted Accounting Principles (GAAP). GAAP look to FASB's hedge accounting rules to determine the proper reporting treatment of financial derivatives for anyone who trades them, whether they are properly classified as hedgers or not. **If you don't meet the hedge accounting criteria, you must report all gains and losses on hedging instruments when they occur, not when the profit or loss on the related commodities is recognized.**

In order to reconcile those results with a more detailed accounting that explains the performance of each program, consider customizing your accounting framework to accommodate both needs. Create a chart of accounts with subaccounts that contain what I'll call "out-of-period" bookings. Out-of-period bookings should contain any mismatches between your "hedging" results and the gains or losses they are designed to protect. Then, you can understand how your hedge programs fare when you look at sufficient detail, but also know the entire company's GAAP-reportable results at the summary level.

Clear financial statement footnotes should then describe the major components of those out-of-period bookings. Some training for those who read your financial statements will help bridge the divide between wild swings in reported earnings and a stable, well-performing hedge program.

Hedge Accounting: To Qualify or Not?

By now, you may be wondering why I even pose the above question, for it appears I've already answered it. You might also be wondering why you should even bother with hedging if the accounting is so challenging. However, accounting requirements should never override sound business practices. Don't let the ominous accounting cloud scare you away from protecting your business's risks. Consider the potential impact of the accounting and take preemptive measures where appropriate.

For any businesses that operate outside of the United States, you'll need to ask what effect the international hedge accounting rules may have.

If you offer employee bonus plans based on reported earnings, you may need to revise your calculation methodology if you will not be qualifying for hedge accounting. You'll not want to incentivize—or penalize—employees based on out-of-period bookings.

Debt covenants can be problematic, too. You may need remedial provisions if you don't qualify as a hedger. Work with your lenders to educate them about your reporting and to achieve benchmarks that are fair, yet will still alert them of cash flow problems on the horizon.

Tax rules are also a relevant consideration. Essentially, the US tax code seems to favor recognizing income on financial derivatives that are closed or expired, whose final profit or loss is definitive. You may find this result differs from GAAP accounting, regardless of whether you qualify as a hedger for financial reporting. Consult with your accounting and tax professionals to assess your situation.

Illustration 19.1

Hedge Accounting: To Qualify or Not?

Or

How much money did you make this year? It all depends...

Company offered a fixed-price program, which it hedged to protect its margin on this quantity	1,000,000
Fixed selling price	$4.00
Commodity price at hedge inception	$3.40
Intended, "locked-in" margin	$0.60
Commodity price at year-end, before any deliveries	$3.00
Decline in commodity price	-$0.40
Mark-to-market adjustment on open futures ($3.00 - $3.40 x 1 million)	-$400,000
Reportable year-one earnings:	
If company qualifies for hedge accounting	$750,000
If company does not qualify for hedge accounting	$350,000
In the following year, company delivered its commitments, and then discontinued its fixed-price program	
Reportable year-two earnings:	
If company qualifies for hedge accounting	$925,000
If company does not qualify for hedge accounting*	$1,325,000
*Mark-to-market adjustment reversed in year-two	
Income taxes disregarded	

You can comply with GAAP whether or not you qualify as a hedger, but the bottom line on your income statement may look much different under the two approaches. In the end, since cash ultimately determines all accounting results, you'll report the same cumulative earnings under either approach, once all hedges have been completed. Yet statements report earnings annually and on an interim basis throughout the year, when hedges and the accounting thereof may be in progress. When you zero in on any reporting period in which a hedge overlaps either the beginning or the end of the period, the earnings reported under the two methods will differ.

Whether or not you choose to pursue hedge accounting treatment, realize that you will face some challenges. If you choose to pursue it, you will incur additional cost and add more complexity to your operation, with no guarantee that this treatment will really tell you what you need to know about your hedging activities. If you choose not to pursue it, you'll need to be prepared to reconcile your GAAP financials to a set of internal reports that will better answer these questions: How did our hedge perform? And what did our business really earn? Let's hope those statements show you've been traveling on flat terrain rather than up and down steep hills.

CHAPTER 20

Next Steps

Of what worth is unapplied knowledge?

Have you developed a new appreciation for your own business risks? By now, you may better understand what those risks are. You may also realize that hedging is not only well within your grasp but that you need to investigate it further. Perhaps you understand the concepts, but you need more direction and hand-holding before you can implement a plan. Here are some ideas on how to proceed. **If you're sensing a need to act, don't ignore it.** Those latent business risks need not keep you awake at night.

1. Discuss matters internally with your operations and finance leaders. Brainstorm on what commodity, debt, currency, or weather risks you really do own. Develop a consensus on the materiality of those risks.

2. Talk with key business partners, industry groups, or peers. Find out what others are doing. Consider whether you could work with any of them to protect your own business's risks.

3. Consult with your vendors who deal with the commodity that poses you risk. Ask them if they have programs that could help shield your business from price or rate risks.

4. Talk with your stakeholders, such as lenders and investors. Inform them of your concerns about financial risk. Find out whether your banking partners have a ready solution to manage the risk.

5. If you already have relationships with insurance companies who may be able to provide products or expertise to help you manage price risks, speak with them, too.

6. Consider hiring an independent consultant to advise you, someone without a conflict of interest. Having that type of independent review from a recognized expert may either substantiate your own concerns or set your mind at ease. Either way, you'll learn more about how to address your risks.

If you can picture any scenario that could cripple—or wipe out—your business, it is time that you looked further into protecting your business interests. **Managing risk is all about stabilizing your business and keeping you financially viable for tomorrow, so that your business can continue generating cash for you.** Don't mortgage your future, or squander your legacy, by ignoring real business risks. Take this opportunity to protect the value of one of your most significant assets. A little peace of mind can go a long way.

Lastly, while the content of this book is still fresh in your mind, I would love to hear your feedback. Please feel free to contact me through the contact page of http://hedging .openroadpress.com. If you have constructive feedback that you think will help other potential readers, I wholeheartedly invite you to leave a review at an online bookseller. If you would like advice on how to begin addressing your hedging challenges, please don't hesitate to contact me at tbishop@openroadpress .com.

GLOSSARY

Backwardated: A term used to describe a futures market with lower prices associated with longer times to delivery. When plotted on a chronological graph with the nearer-term months to the left and the outer months to the right, a line connecting the plot points will decline from left to right. The opposite of a backwardated market is a contango market.

Basis: Any of a number of differences between two price indices for the same or a similar commodity. Those differences relate primarily to time, location, or product specification.

Capacity: The ability of a business to service a certain amount of customer demand for its products and services due to its size and operating infrastructure.

Clearing member firm: A company that belongs to a regulated futures exchange. A clearing member firm typically has the capital investment and financial wherewithal to provide financial strength to the exchange, while managing the credit risk and cash flows of various brokers' trading clients who utilize it.

Commodity: A staple used in many businesses and subject to significant price fluctuations due to the effects of global supply and demand. Examples of commodities are cocoa, coffee, sugar, milk, orange juice, cattle, wheat, corn, soybeans, natural gas, crude oil, gasoline, electricity, platinum, gold, and silver.

Commodity price risk: A condition that exists when an adverse change in the price of a commodity would reduce the net worth of a business.

Contango: A term used to describe a futures market with higher prices associated with longer times to delivery. When plotted on a chronological graph with the nearer-term months to the left and the outer months to the right, a line connecting the plot points will rise from left to right. The opposite of a contango market is a backwardated market.

Contribution margin: See Margin, contribution.

Counterparty risk: The risk associated with a trading partner's creditworthiness or ability to perform.

Currency exchange rate: A factor used to convert from a value in one country's currency to a value in another country's currency.

Debt, fixed-rate: A borrowing with interest cost determined by an interest rate that does not vary.

Debt, variable-rate: A borrowing with interest cost determined by an interest rate that fluctuates with the market.

Debt amortization: The rate at which the principal balance of a borrowing is reduced by the borrower's periodic payments.

Debt capital: A source of a business's funding that comes from outside parties, the cost of which is assessed as interest expense.

Debt principal: The amount of money owed to a lender.

Debt term: The duration of a borrowing.

Derivative, financial: A futures contract, swap agreement, or any option thereon, or any other financially settled contract whose value is derived from changes in the price of a commodity or other index. Synonymous with financial instrument.

Derivative, weather: A financial derivative the payout for which is premised on changes in weather rather than changes in the price of another commodity or other index. The unit of measure in a weather derivative is usually based on precipitation or temperature.

Fixed costs: Costs that do not vary with sales. A business generates contribution margin through sales to cover its fixed costs, and then to compensate its owners.

Fixed forward contract: An agreement whereby a supplier agrees to sell to a buyer a specified quantity of a specified commodity for delivery at a specified future time and location at a cost that is fixed when the contract is executed.

Futures contract: An agreement to effect delivery of a specified quantity of a specified commodity at a specified time and location. When one enters into a position to either take or make delivery, the price at which delivery will be transacted becomes specified. See this CMEGroup webpage for the specifications for a crude oil futures contract: http://www.cmegroup.com/trading/energy/crude-oil/light-sweet-crude_contract_specifications.html.

Futures exchange: An organization that governs the buying and selling of commodities for delivery in future months. An exchange establishes standards for contracts, market participants, and cash flows between participants.

Futures market: An aggregation of traders willing to commit to delivering, or accepting delivery of, a commodity in a future month at a specified price, even if such commitments will not result in physical delivery due to pre-delivery cancellation of the futures contracts or trading a financial derivative designed to avoid delivery.

Hedger: One who seeks to reduce risk by transferring it to others, usually by trading financial derivatives, by purchasing insurance, or by negotiating contract provisions with business partners.

Hedging: Transfer of risk to others, usually by trading financial derivatives, by purchasing insurance, or by negotiating contract provisions with business partners.

Instrument, financial: See Derivative, financial.

Intrinsic value: A portion of an option's value comprised of any positive value that would result in its underlying futures contract if the option were immediately exercised. For example, a crude oil December call option with a $100 strike price has a $2 intrinsic value when the December crude oil futures contract is trading at $102.

ISDA master agreement: Legal contract that governs the trading of over-the-counter swaps, typically signed by two parties who intend to trade with one another. ISDA stands for International Swaps and Derivatives Association, Inc. For further information, see http://www2.isda.org/about-isda/.

Liquidity: A market phenomenon that allows participants to transact at will because there are enough participants willing to take the other side of any trade at any time.

Margin, contribution: Sales minus their associated variable costs. A company breaks even when its total contribution margin equals its total fixed costs.

Margin, profit: As used in this book, the difference between the sales of a commodity and its cost, inclusive of hedging gains and losses on that commodity.

Margin, trading: Collateral, usually cash, required to secure an open position in a futures market. For example, here are CMEGroup's margin requirements for gold: http://www.cmegroup.com/trading/metals/precious/gold_performance_bonds.html.

Offset: When a long and a short position in futures contracts of the same commodity and in the same quantity and delivery month eliminate one another. Offset results in nullifying any commitment to effect delivery under such contracts and finalizing the gain or loss on such contracts. Identical option contracts are offset in the same manner.

Opportunity cost: The unknown cost of willingly forgoing a potential benefit in a business decision.

Option: A financial instrument that conveys to its holder the right, but not the obligation, to acquire a position in the underlying futures contract or swap agreement at a price equal to the option's strike price.

Option – Call: A financial instrument that conveys to its holder the right, but not the obligation, to acquire a long position in the underlying futures contract or swap agreement at a price equal to the option's strike price.

Option – Put: A financial instrument that conveys to its holder the right, but not the obligation, to acquire a short position in the underlying futures contract or swap agreement at a price equal to the option's strike price.

Over-the-counter market: Any futures market that does not trade on a regulated exchange.

Owner capital: A source of business funding from its owner, whether infusion of cash or assets (without an obligation to repay) or retention of accumulated earnings, collectively referred to as shareholders' equity.

Physical market: An aggregation of buyers and sellers of the same commodity for delivery at a specific time and location in exchange for cash.

Position (or holding a position): Anyone who buys or sells futures or option contracts holds a position in the market (unless that transaction is used to offset an existing position).

Position – Long: A long futures or options position results from buying any number of the same contract, provided such purchase does not offset a short position. A long position will need to be offset before the expiration of the contract in order to close it. A long position is offset by entering into a trade to sell the same contract in the same quantity.

Position – Short: A short futures or options position results from selling any number of the same contract, provided such sale does not offset a long position. A short position will need to be offset before the expiration of the contract in order to close it. A short position is offset by entering into a trade to buy the same contract in the same quantity.

Price correlation: The comparison of the rate of price change in a hedging instrument with the rate of price change in the physical product being hedged.

Price discovery: A term acknowledging that the price of a specified commodity to be delivered at a specified place and at a specified time in the future is readily available to anyone who watches the futures market. This CMEGroup webpage shows how much corn is worth in the future: http://www.cmegroup.com/trading/agricultural/grain-and-oilseed/corn.html.

Profit margin: See Margin, profit.

Speculation: Trading in financial instruments without already having a price risk to hedge. Speculation is diametrically opposed to hedging because it increases risk rather than reducing it.

Strike price: A preset price assigned to an option that allows the option's holder to acquire a position in the option's underlying futures contract or swap agreement at such price.

Strip: A set of contiguous months with a shared commodity price risk. In hedging, a strip can be traded or settled as one instrument or as a series of instruments for the individual months that comprise it.

Swap agreement: A financial instrument traded over the counter in lieu of a futures contract traded on a regulated exchange. Each of the two parties to a swap agrees to a swap level, usually a price. When the swap settles, one party benefits at the expense of the other on any deviation of the price or other index from the agreed-upon swap level, as determined by the original agreement. A swap is always settled financially.

Variable costs: Costs that vary with sales. Variable costs are compared to sales to determine contribution margin.

Weather derivative: See Derivative, weather.

INDEX

T

V

W

LIST OF WEBSITE ADDRESSES

The following list provides the complete addresses (URLs) to website links found in the e-book version of *Hedging Demystified*.

CMEGroup home webpage:
http://www.cmegroup.com/

Profile of the book's editor, Sandra J. Judd:
https://www.linkedin.com/in/sandy-judd-a1576ab/

CMEGroup contract specifications for Chicago #2 soft red winter wheat:
http://www.cmegroup.com/trading/agricultural/grain-and-oilseed/wheat_contract_specifications.html

CMEGroup actual trades of gasoline futures:
http://www.cmegroup.com/trading/energy/refined-products/rbob-gasoline_quotes_timeSales_globex_futures.html

Current clearing members of the CMEGroup:
http://www.cmegroup.com/tools-information/clearing-firms.html

CMEGroup contract specifications for live cattle:
http://www.cmegroup.com/trading/agricultural/livestock/live-cattle_contract_specifications.html

CMEGroup actual trades of live cattle futures:
https://www.cmegroup.com/trading/agricultural/livestock/live-cattle.html

CMEGroup margin requirements for gold contract:
http://www.cmegroup.com/trading/metals/precious/gold_performance_bonds.html

CMEGroup daily settlement prices for gasoline:
http://www.cmegroup.com/trading/energy/refined-products/rbob-gasoline_quotes_settlements_futures.html

CMEGroup monthly prices for corn:
http://www.cmegroup.com/trading/agricultural/grain-and-oilseed/corn.html

Option styles:
http://en.wikipedia.org/wiki/Option_style

Black-76 option-pricing model:
http://en.wikipedia.org/wiki/Black_model

Explanation of LIBOR:
http://en.wikipedia.org/wiki/Libor

CMEGroup price quotes for CAD/USD foreign exchange contract:
http://www.cmegroup.com/trading/fx/g10/canadian-dollar_quotes_globex.html

CMEGroup contract specifications for CAD/USD foreign exchange rate:
http://www.cmegroup.com/trading/fx/g10/canadian-dollar_contract_specifications.html

Explanation of El Nino:
http://en.wikipedia.org/wiki/El_Ni%C3%B1o

Explanation of La Nina:
http://en.wikipedia.org/wiki/La_Ni%C3%B1a

Financial Accounting Standards Board website:
http://www.fasb.org/

International Financial Reporting Standards (and their International Accounting Standards Board) website:
https://www.ifrs.org/issued-standards/list-of-standards/

CMEGroup contract specifications for crude oil:
http://www.cmegroup.com/trading/energy/crude-oil/light-sweet-crude_contract_specifications.html

International Swaps and Derivatives Association website:
http://www2.isda.org/about-isda/

ACKNOWLEDGMENTS

You cannot publish a book like this with any reasonable level of quality without input from others. I'm grateful to the following individuals who reviewed preliminary versions of this book and provided helpful feedback and encouragement: Alan Dorr, Bob Moore, Bob Strong, Charlie Hahn, Dan Thornton, Dave Trapp, David Flanagan, David Harbison, Dick Roderick, Fred Ludwig, Heather Bergeron, Jane Parker, Joe Smith, Jordan Ness, Kathy McHenry, Kevin Mikoski, Levi Ross, Lloyd Porter, Marty White, Matt Borden, Mike Porter, Paul Hoyt, Randy Bishop, Steve Bishop, and Tim Malikowski. Levi Ross deserves credit for his ingenuity in "demystifying" the main title. Thank you all for your time and your contributions. I could not have done this without your help.

Steve Bishop could also have been dubbed "editor-in-chief" for the content on this project. I've found there's a benefit to working with family. You don't have any difficulty understanding what they think of your work! Steve has years of experience in business finance. He read and reread copy after copy and provided relevant and direct feedback at every turn, which prompted many revisions. Steve, your contributions were invaluable to the success of this project. Thank you.

Thank you, as well, to Sandy Judd, for her professional copyediting. It's not easy editing a book about such a technical topic, but, true to her word, Sandy was not intimidated by any of the content.

And a special thanks to Joe Smith for lending his years of expertise on hedging. Joe wrote the foreword, in which he explains why hedging is important and what readers can expect when they look deeper into this book.

ABOUT THE AUTHOR

With over thirty years of business experience, Tim Bishop has seen hedging from all angles. He designed, implemented, and executed a hedging program for a multimillion-dollar heating oil distributor. He devised hedging strategies, developed hedging partner relationships, initiated trades, and supervised the accounting for fourteen years. As company treasurer, he was responsible for not only cash management and reporting but also compliance with financial reporting standards, tax law, and debt covenants.

As one who regularly reported to both an outside board of directors and a management team, he understands the challenges of communicating complex information to a multidisciplinary group of professionals who do not live and breathe hedging concepts. He also served as a director of the company's primary commodity storage facility, so he appreciates the operational considerations of managing risk. Add in Tim's background as a tax accountant and a CPA, and you have someone fully qualified to speak the languages of all parties who touch commodity price risk management.

In addition to consulting for small businesses, Tim Bishop has co-authored books with his wife, Debbie, about their midlife launch into both marriage and cross-country bicycle touring. *Two Are Better: Midlife Newlyweds Bicycle Coast to Coast* captures the story behind the story, while *Bicycle Touring How-To: What We Learned* shares their knowledge with bicycle touring wannabes. Tim serves as a volunteer hope coach for TheHopeLine, a nonprofit organization that seeks to reach, rescue, and restore hurting teens and young adults. He blogs periodically at www.openroadpress.com.

ABOUT OPEN ROAD PRESS

What you do get when you combine faith, life experience, second chances, and thousands of miles of self-supported bicycle touring throughout America?

Inspiration • Hope • Encouragement

Adventure • Fun • Entertainment

   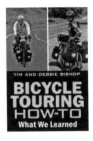

You also get uplifting books that share the journey and what it teaches the willing traveler, including an eight-time award winner. *Wheels of Wisdom: Life Lessons for the Restless Spirit* has won four first-place book awards–in Inspiration, Devotional, Christian Nonfiction, and Christian Inspirational. Publishers Weekly dubbed it "a road map for life."

Check out our books at openroadpress.com. Take up the challenge to make meaning and adventure vital parts of your daily life.

OPEN ROAD PRESS

Open Road Press • Love and Life by Bicycle

Questions, comments, and feedback are always welcome at openroadpress.com. We will do our best to respond to all constructive comments and questions.